Scottish Tales of
Magic & Mystery

Scottish Tales of Magic & Mystery

compiled by
Marion Lochhead
and illustrated by
James Hutcheson

Johnston and Bacon
London and Edinburgh

A Johnston & Bacon book published by Cassell Ltd.
35 Red Lion Square, London WC1R 4SG
& Tanfield House, Tanfield Lane, Edinburgh EH3 5LL
and at Sydney, Auckland, Toronto, Johannesburg,
an affiliate of
Macmillan Publishing Co.
New York

© Johnston & Bacon,
a division of Cassell Ltd., 1978

First published 1978

ISBN 0 7179 4248 1

Typeset by Inforum Ltd.,
Portsmouth
Printed and bound in Great Britain by
Hazell Watson & Viney Ltd,
Aylesbury, Bucks

Contents

Acknowledgements

For permission to include copyright material acknowledgements are made to the following: to the author and The Hogarth Press Ltd for *The Seal King* from *The Two Fiddlers* by George Mackay Brown; to Souvenir Press Ltd for *Machinery* from *Young Art and Old Hector* by Neil M. Gunn; to the estate of the late Susan Lady Tweedsmuir and Hodder & Stoughton Ltd for an extract from *Witch Wood* by John Buchan.

Every effort has been made to trace copyright holders. Where this has not been possible, the publishers wish to tender their apologies and thanks.

Introduction

The Scot is a complex character, with more in him than is conveyed by the common adjectives canny and pawky or by the music-hall image in kilt and bonnet singing comic or sentimental songs. There is also the grave, industrious Scot with no apparent tendency towards folly or fancy; there is the soldier, the explorer, the wanderer to the furthest rim of the earth. But even beyond, or perhaps within the wanderer there is another, a hidden Scot. He may not wander far from his country, or even from his parish, he may go soberly about his affairs, but he has explored that Other Country, the hidden realm of Scotland where strange things are seen.

This Scot is a borderer not merely in the geographical sense (although he is often found on the Borders); the borderland he visits is beyond this world. It may be very near heaven or very near hell; often it is the country of magic, Elfhame, the realm of the fairies or the Good People as it is prudent and courteous to call them; the place which one of those wandering Scots called The Secret Commonwealth of Elves, Fauns and Fairies. There is also the darker region of wizardry, and beyond that the boundary of hell itself.

This latter province was well known to the Border Scot — in the strict geographical meaning. Sir Walter Scott wrote of it and so did his friend and contemporary, James Hogg; Robert Louis Stevenson knew it (though not a Borderer he was of the south, and Edinburgh, his native city, lies very close to Scott country); John Buchan discovered it and brought back strange tidings.

In the north, in the Highlands and Islands, the discovery is rather of fairies and of sea-magic, of spells and the rescue of the spellbound; yet this cannot be made a strict distinction. Hogg, who wrote so uncannily well about the devil and his adherents, also wrote of paradise in his poem

Kilmeny, *and two of the greatest Border ballads,* Thomas the Rhymer *and* Tam Lin, *deal with the taking of mortals into Elfhame.*

The diversity of that other country is even greater than the diversity of this visible world and the discoveries of the wandering Scot are manifold.

The peculiar fascination of this fellow lies in his dual existence. He has a remarkable capacity for leading an ordinary life, as a solid, respectable citizen, a good countryman, a man of law or letters, a cleric, an administrator. The authors from whom these tales have come were all of this sort, at home in this world of common humanity.

There are indeed few things in heaven and on earth and in the regions in between that have not been contemplated by the Scottish imagination. Our wanderer has been aware of a holiness beyond ordinary decency, an evil darker than mere disreputable weakness, and above all, of a strange neutrality, neither black nor white, but a shadowy and glimmering grey where danger lurks and allures the soul into strange realms.

The peril was not only for mortals who entered or were drawn into that place of shadows, dreams, illusions, and enchantments. The elves and fairies were, by some accounts, bound to pay a tiend or tax of one of their own kind to hell; if they could substitute a human victim, so much the better. A kidnapped human soul was a rich tribute to the kingdom of darkness.

It may be added that the phrase 'he is away with the fairies' is often used, by people of no turn for fantasy, to describe someone of slightly wandering wits or temporary aberration.

One of the most entrancing clerics who ever lived was the Reverend Robert Kirk (1641-92), minister of the parish of Aberfoyle in Perthshire. He was a graduate of Edinburgh and St Andrew's universities, a Gaelic scholar, and he wrote that unique masterpiece, The Secret Commonwealth of Elves, Fauns and Fairies. *This was left in manuscript for more than a century after his death — or departure from this earth. He knew a great deal, perhaps too much, about those Other People, and in the end they took him.*

Sir Walter Scott visited Aberfoyle, saw the grave and the tombstone which records his death, and wrote this account in his Letters on Demonology and Witchcraft:

The Reverend Robert Kirke was, in the end of the seventeenth century, successively minister of the Highland parishes of Balquidder and Aberfoyle, lying in the most romantic district of Perthshire, and within the Highland line. These beautiful and wild regions, comprehending so many lakes, rocks, sequestered valleys, and dim copsewoods, are not even yet quite abandoned by the fairies, who have resolutely maintained secure footing in a region so well suited for their residence. Indeed, so much was this the case formerly, that Mr. Kirke, while in his latter charge of Aberfoyle, found materials for collecting and compiling his Essay on the "Subterranean and for the most part Invisible People heretofore going under the name of Elves, Fawnes, and Fairies, or the like." In this discourse, the author, "with undoubting mind," describes the fairy race as a sort of astral spirits, of a kind betwixt humanity and angels — says, that they have children, nurses, marriages, deaths, and burials, like mortals in appearance; that, in some respect, they represent mortal men, and that individual apparitions, or double-men, are found among them, corresponding with

3

mortals existing on earth. Mr. Kirke accuses them of
stealing the milk from the cows, and of carrying away, what
is more material, the women in pregnancy, and new-born
children from their nurses. The remedy is easy in both cases.
The milk cannot be stolen if the mouth of the calf, before he
is permitted to suck, be rubbed with a certain balsam, very
easily come by; and the woman in travail is safe if a piece of
cold iron is put into the bed. Mr. Kirke accounts for this by
informing us that the great northern mines of iron, lying
adjacent to the place of eternal punishment, have a savour
odious to these "fascinating creatures." They have, says the
reverend author, what one would not expect, many light
toyish books (novels and plays, doubtless), others on
Rosycrucian subjects, and of an abstruse mystical character;
but they have no Bibles or works of devotion. The essayist
fails not to mention the elf-arrow heads, which have
something of the subtlety of thunderbolts, and can mortally
wound the vital parts without breaking the skin. These
wounds, he says, he has himself observed in beasts, and felt
the fatal lacerations which he could not see.

It was by no means to be supposed that the elves, so
jealous and irritable a race as to be incensed against those
who spoke of them under their proper names, should be less
than mortally offended at the temerity of the reverend
author, who had pryed so deeply into their mysteries, for the
purpose of giving them to the public. Although, therefore,
the learned divine's monument, with the name duly
inscribed, is to be seen at the east end of the churchyard at
Aberfoyle, yet those acquainted with his real history do not
believe that he enjoys the natural repose of the tomb. His
successor, the Rev. Dr. Grahame, has informed us of the
general belief that, as Mr. Kirke was walking one evening in
his night-gown upon a *Dun-shi*, or fairy mount, in the
vicinity of the manse or parsonage, behold! he sunk down in
what seemed to be a fit of apoplexy, which the
unenlightened took for death, while the more understanding
knew it to be a swoon produced by the supernatural
influence of the people whose precincts he had violated.
After the ceremony of a seeming funeral, the form of the
Rev. Robert Kirke appeared to a relation, and commanded

4

him to go to Grahame of Duchray, ancestor of the present
General Graham Stirling. "Say to Duchray, who is my
cousin as well as your own, that I am not dead, but a captive
in Fairyland, and only one chance remains for my
liberation. When the posthumous child, of which my wife
has been delivered since my disappearance, shall be brought
to baptism, I will appear in the room, when, if Duchray shall
throw over my head the knife or dirk which he holds in his
hand, I may be restored to society; but if this opportunity is
neglected, I am lost for ever." Duchray was apprised of what
was to be done. The ceremony took place, and the
apparition of Mr. Kirke was visibly seen while they were
seated at table; but Grahame of Duchray, in his
astonishment, failed to perform the ceremony enjoined, and
it is to be feared that Mr. Kirke still "drees his weird in
Fairyland," the Elfin state declaring to him, as the Ocean to
poor Falconer, who perished at sea after having written his
popular poem of "The Shipwreck" —

"Thou hast proclaimed our power — be thou our prey!"

*And now for Mr Kirk's own narrative of the 'Subterranean
Inhabitants'.*

These *Siths*, or FAIRIES, they call *Sleagh Maith*, or the
Good People, it would seem, to prevent the Dint of their ill
Attempts, (for the Irish use to bless all they fear Harme of;)
and are said to be of a midle Nature betuixt Man and Angel,
as were Daemons thought to be of old; of intelligent
studious Spirits, and light changable Bodies (lyke those
called Astral), somewhat of the Nature of a condensed
Cloud, and best seen in Twilight. Thes Bodies be so plyable
thorough the Subtilty of the Spirits that agitate them, that
they can make them appear or disappear att Pleasure. Some
have Bodies or Vehicles so spungious, thin, and desecat, that
they are fed by only sucking into some fine spirituous
Liquors, that peirce lyke pure Air and Oyl: other feid more
gross on the Foyson or substance of Corns and Liquors, or
Corne it selfe that grows on the Surface of the Earth, which
these Fairies steall away, partly invisible, partly preying on

5

the Grain, as do Crowes and Mice; wherefore in this same Age, they are some times heard to bake Bread, strike Hammers, and do such lyke Services within the little Hillocks they most haunt: some whereof of old, before the Gospell dispelled Paganism, and in some barbarous Places as yet, enter Houses after all are at rest, and set the Kitchens in order, cleansing all the Vessels. Such Drags goe under the name of Brownies. When we have plenty, they have Scarcity at their Homes; and on the contrarie (for they are empowred to catch as much Prey everywhere as they please), there Robberies notwithstanding oft tymes occassion great Rickes of Corne not to bleed so weill, (as they call it,) or prove so copious by verie farr as wes expected by the Owner. .... They are said to have aristocraticall Rulers and Laws, but no discernible Religion, Love, or Devotion towards God, the blessed Maker of all: they disappear whenever they hear his Name invocked, or the Name of JESUS, (at which all do bow willinglie, or by constraint, that dwell above or beneath within the Earth, Philip. 2. 10;) nor can they act ought at that Time after hearing of that sacred Name.

This note recurs in fairy lore. The Holy Name guards those who speak it in reverence and in prayer; but terrifies those who have rejected God as the fallen angels did, and those who are not of heaven or earth or hell but some region between, like the siths *or fairies.*

The Reverend Robert Wodrow (1679-1734) had better luck than Mr Kirk, his life ending in natural death. He too was a scholar and Quaestor or Librarian of Glasgow College Library, where he wrote many letters reflecting the intellectual life of his time. His major and most fascinating work was The Analecta, or Materials for a History of Remarkable Providences, mostly relating to Scotch Ministers and Christians. *These included some strange encounters, not with elves, fauns and fairies, but with the devil himself; as was the experience of Mr James Lochhead:*

6

The little Hillocks they most haunt

This night James Lochhead told me that last year ...
at the Communion of Balfron he was much helped, all
day. At night, when dark somewhat he went out to the feilds
to pray; and a terrible, slavish fear came on him, that he
almost lost his senses. Houever, he resolved to goe on to his
duty. By the time he was at the place, his fear was off him;
and, lying on a knou-side*, a black dogg came to his side and
stood. He said he kneu it to be Satan, and shooke his hand,
but for nothing, it evanishing. He went on in prayer, with as
great enlargment if not greater, than ever. When he ended,
the dogg was ther, and he was not a whit moved. When he
moved, it evanished; and he came home to his quarters in a
very composed frame. He told me, that at another time, at
the Table, he was very weel (as he expressed it) and ther
came a flash in his face which quite discomposed him. He
looked on it as from Satan for he enquired at severall at the
Table and elswher if they noticed it, which they said they did
not. Lord help us against his devices, and strenthen against
them.

*Sir Walter Scott (1771-1832) was one of the most complex
as well as the greatest of Scotsmen. An eminent lawyer,
Clerk to the Court of Session, Sheriff of Selkirk, Laird of
Abbotsford, he won European fame as poet and novelist. In
both these functions he showed his genius for narrative, his
capacity to bring history to life; and in some of his poems
and some of his characters he revealed that inner self, that
knowledge of the Other Country of magic and mystery. One
of his greatest stories and one of the best in Scottish
literature is* Wandering Willie's Tale, *found in* Redgauntlet,
*in which Wandering Willie tells how his grandfather went to
hell to find his departed laird and have from him a receipt
for rent duly paid — the lawyer as well as the story-teller had
a hand in this!*

*a knoll

A black dogg came to his side

In his introduction to the Letters on Demonology and Witchcraft *Scott wrote: 'Among much reading of my earlier days . . . I have travelled a good deal in the twilight regions of superstitious disquisitions' — of which these* Letters *give examples. The more one reads of Scott the more one realises that he was lucky to escape the fate of Mr Kirk. The 'Wizard of the North', to give him that most appropriate title, came near knowing too much.*

The employment, the benefits, the amusements of the Fairy court, resembled the aerial people themselves. Their government was always represented as monarchical. A King, more frequently a Queen of Fairies, was acknowledged; and sometimes both held their court together. Their pageants and court entertainments comprehended all that the imagination could conceive of what was, by that age, accounted gallant and splendid. At their processions they paraded more beautiful steeds than those of mere earthly parentage — the hawks and hounds which they employed in their chase were of the first race. At their daily banquets, the board was set forth with a splendour which the proudest kings of the earth dared not aspire to; and the hall of their dancers echoed to the most exquisite music. But when viewed by the eye of a seer the illusion vanished. The young knights and beautiful ladies showed themselves as wrinkled carles and odious hags — their wealth turned into slate-stones — the splendid plate into pieces of clay fantastically twisted — and their victuals, unsavoured by salt (prohibited to them, we are told, because an emblem of eternity), became tasteless and insipid — the stately halls were turned into miserable damp caverns — all the delights of the Elfin Elysium vanished at once. In a word, their pleasures were showy, but totally unsubstantial — their activity unceasing, but fruitless and unavailing — and their condemnation appears to have consisted in the necessity of maintaining the appearance of constant industry or enjoyment, though their toil was fruitless and their pleasures shadowy and unsubstantial. Hence poets have designed them as "*the crew that never rest.*" Besides the unceasing and useless bustle in which these spirits seemed to live, they had propensities unfavourable and distressing to mortals.

One injury of a very serious nature was supposed to be constantly practised by the fairies against "the human mortals," that of carrying off their children, and breeding them as beings of their race. Unchristened infants were chiefly exposed to this calamity, but adults were also liable to be abstracted from earthly commerce, notwithstanding it was their natural sphere. With respect to the first, it may be easily conceived that the want of the sacred ceremony of introduction into the Christian church rendered them the more obnoxious to the power of those creatures, who, if not to be in all respects considered as fiends, had nevertheless, considering their constant round of idle occupation, little right to rank themselves among good spirits, and were accounted by most divines as belonging to a very different class. An adult, on the other hand, must have been engaged in some action which exposed him to the power of the spirits, and so, as the legal phrase went, "taken in the manner." Sleeping on a fairy mount, within which the Fairy court happened to be held for the time, was a very ready mode of obtaining a pass for Elfland. It was well for the individual if the irate elves were contented, on such occasions, with transporting him through the air to a city at some forty miles' distance, and leaving, perhaps, his hat or bonnet on some steeple between, to mark the direct line of his course. Others, when engaged in some unlawful action, or in the act of giving way to some headlong and sinful passion, exposed themselves also to become inmates of Fairyland.

Of the custom called 'the gudeman's croft' Scott writes:

In many parishes of Scotland there was suffered to exist a certain portion of land, called *the gudeman's croft*, which was never ploughed or cultivated, but suffered to remain waste ... Though it was not expressly avowed, no one doubted that "the goodman's croft" was set apart for some evil being; in fact, that it was the portion of the arch-fiend

11

The irate elves transported him through the air

himself, whom our ancestors distinguished by a name which, while it was generally understood, could not, it was supposed, be offensive to the stern inhabitant of the regions of despair. This was so general a custom that the Church published an ordinance against it as an impious and blasphemous usage.

This singular custom sunk before the efforts of the clergy in the seventeenth century; but there must still be many alive who, in childhood, have been taught to look with wonder on knolls and patches of ground left uncultivated, because, whenever a ploughshare entered the soil, the elementary spirits were supposed to testify their displeasure by storm and thunder.

The name, 'the gudeman', was propitiatory, like that of the Good People for the fairies. Speak well of all men, and of other beings too, even the worst of them, and take due measures against them.

A variety of such names has been bestowed by canny Scots upon the devil: Auld Nick, Auld Hornie, Auld Cloutie (cloven-hoof).

Scott returns to the lure of Elfhame in many of his Letters. Thomas of Erceldoune — His Amour with the Queen of Elfland *is a moral tale (and morality occurs frequently in fairy lore): presumption is a sin to be punished.*

Thomas of Erceldoune, in Lauderdale, called the Rhymer on account of his producing a poetical romance on the subject of Tristrem and Yseult, which is curious as the earliest specimen of English verse known to exist, flourished in the reign of Alexander III. of Scotland. Like other men of talent of the period, Thomas was suspected of magic. He was said also to have the gift of prophecy, which was accounted for in the following peculiar manner, referring entirely to the elfin superstition: — As True Thomas (we give him the epithet by anticipation) lay on Huntly Bank, a

13

place on the descent of the Eildon Hills, which raise their triple crest above the celebrated Monastery of Melrose, he saw a lady so extremely beautiful that he imagined it must be the Virgin Mary herself. Her appointments, however, were rather those of an Amazon or goddess of the woods. Her steed was of the highest beauty and spirit, and at his mane hung thirty silver bells and nine, which made music to the wind as she paced along. Her saddle was of *royal bone* (ivory), laid over with *orfeverie* — *i.e.*, goldsmith's work. Her stirrups, her dress, all corresponded with her extreme beauty and the magnificence of her array. The fair huntress had her bow in her hand, and her arrows at her belt. She led three greyhounds in a leash, and three raches, or hounds of scent, followed her closely. She rejected and disclaimed the homage which Thomas desired to pay to her; so that, passing from one extremity to the other, Thomas became as bold as he had at first been humble. The lady warns him that he must become her slave if he should prosecute his suit towards her in the manner he proposes. Before their interview terminates, the appearance of the beautiful lady is changed into that of the most hideous hag in existence. One side is blighted and wasted, as if by palsy; one eye drops from her head; her colour, as clear as the virgin silver, is now of a dun leaden hue. A witch from the spital or almshouse would have been a goddess in comparison to the late beautiful huntress. Hideous as she was, Thomas's irregular desires had placed him under the control of this hag, and when she bade him take leave of sun, and of the leaf that grew on tree, he felt himself under the necessity of obeying her. A cavern received them, in which, following his frightful guide, he for three days travelled in darkness, sometimes hearing the booming of a distant ocean, sometimes walking through rivers of blood, which crossed their subterranean path. At length they emerged into daylight, in a most beautiful orchard. Thomas, almost fainting for want of food, stretches out his hand towards the goodly fruit which hangs around him, but is forbidden by his conductress, who informs him these are the fatal apples which were the cause of the fall of man. He perceives also that his guide had no sooner entered this mysterious ground,

14

He saw a lady so extremely beautiful

and breathed its magic air, than she was revived in beauty, equipage, and splendour, as fair, or fairer, than he had first seen her on the mountain. She then commands him to lay his head upon her knee, and proceeds to explain to him the character of the country. "Yonder right-hand path," she says, "conveys the spirits of the blessed to Paradise; yon downward and well-worn way leads sinful souls to the place of everlasting punishment; the third road by yonder dark brake conducts to the milder place of pain from which prayer and mass may release offenders. But see you yet a fourth road, sweeping along the plain to yonder splendid castle? Yonder is the road to Elfland, to which we are now bound. The lord of the castle is king of the country, and I am his queen. But, Thomas, I would rather be drawn with wild horses, than he should know what hath passed between you and me. Therefore, when we enter yonder castle, observe strict silence, and answer no question that is asked at you, and I will account for your silence by saying I took your speech when I brought you from middle earth."

Having thus instructed her lover, they journeyed on to the castle, and entering by the kitchen, found themselves in the midst of such a festive scene as might become the mansion of a great feudal lord or prince. Thirty carcases of deer were lying on the massive kitchen board, under the hands of numerous cooks, who toiled to cut them up and dress them, while the gigantic greyhounds which had taken the spoil lay lapping the blood, and enjoying the sight of the slain game. They came next to the royal hall, where the king received his loving consort without censure or suspicion. Knights and ladies, dancing by threes (reels perhaps), occupied the floor of the hall, and Thomas, the fatigues of his journey from the Eildon hills forgotten, went forward and joined in the revelry. After a period, however, which seemed to him a very short one, the queen spoke with him apart, and bade him prepare to return to his own country. "Now," said the queen, "how long think you that you have been here?" "Certes, fair lady," answered Thomas, "not above these seven days." "You are deceived," answered the queen, "you have been seven *years* in this castle; and it is full time you were gone. Know, Thomas, that the fiend of hell will come to this castle to-morrow to demand his tribute, and so handsome a man as you will attract his eye. For all the world would I not suffer you to be betrayed to such a fate; therefore up, and let us be going." These terrible news reconciled Thomas to his departure from Elfin land, and the queen was not long in placing him upon Huntly bank, where the birds were singing. She took a tender leave of him, and to ensure his reputation, bestowed on him the tongue which *could not lie*. Thomas in vain objected to this inconvenient and involuntary adhesion to veracity, which would make him, as he thought, unfit for church or for market, for king's court or for lady's bower. But all his remonstrances were disregarded by the lady, and Thomas the Rhymer, whenever the discourse turned on the future, gained the credit of a prophet whether he would or not; for he could say nothing but what was sure to come to pass. It is plain that had Thomas been a legislator instead of a poet, we have here the story of Numa and Egeria.

Thomas remained several years in his own tower near Erceldoune, and enjoyed the fame of his predictions, several of which are current among the country people to this day. At length, as the prophet was entertaining the Earl of March in his dwelling, a cry of astonishment arose in the village, on the appearance of a hart and hind, which left the forest and, contrary to their shy nature, came quietly onward, traversing the village towards the dwelling of Thomas. The prophet instantly rose from the board; and, acknowledging the prodigy as the summons of his fate, he accompanied the hart and hind into the forest, and though occasionally seen by individuals to whom he has chosen to show himself, has never again mixed familiarly with mankind.

Thomas of Erceldoune, during his retirement, has been supposed, from time to time, to be levying forces to take the field in some crisis of his country's fate. The story has often been told of a daring horse-jockey having sold a black horse to a man of venerable and antique appearance, who appointed the remarkable hillock upon Eildon hills, called the Lucken-hare, as the place where, at twelve o'clock at night, he should receive the price. He came, his money was paid in ancient coin, and he was invited by his customer to

17

view his residence. The trader in horses followed his guide in the deepest astonishment through several long ranges of stalls, in each of which a horse stood motionless, while an armed warrior lay equally still at the charger's feet. "All these men," said the wizard in a whisper, "will awaken at the battle of Sheriffmoor." At the extremity of this extraordinary depôt hung a sword and a horn, which the prophet pointed out to the horse-dealer as containing the means of dissolving the spell. The man in confusion took the horn, and attempted to wind it. The horses instantly started in their stalls, stamped, and shook their bridles, the men arose and clashed their armour, and the mortal, terrified at the tumult he had excited, dropped the horn from his hand. A voice like that of a giant, louder even than the tumult around, pronounced these words: —

"Woe to the coward that ever he was born,
That did not draw the sword before he blew the horn!"

A whirlwind expelled the horse-dealer from the cavern, the entrance to which he could never again find.

James Hogg (1771-1837), known as the Ettrick Shepherd, was a friend and contemporary of Scott. He was from his boyhood a shepherd in Ettrick dale, and wrote besides his poems and stories of fairies, witches and demons, a treatise on the Diseases of Sheep *which was for years a near best-seller. His range of magic included the lovely poem,* Kilmeny, *which has more than a gleam of holiness, a riotous poem about* The Witch of Fife, *and that terrifying masterpiece,* Confessions of a Justified Sinner, *in which the narrator encounters the devil and is captivated.*

Hogg had little schooling. He learned to read and write and continued to teach himself, reading everything he could lay hands on; and listening to his mother's tales and ballads which she had heard from her father. Hogg's mother once recited a ballad to Scott which he used in his Border Minstrelsy *and was, for this, sternly rebuked by her. These*

18

poems and ballads were meant to be said, *not set down in print; and in his* Minstrelsy *they 'were neither richt set doun nor richt printed'. Scott took it meekly.*

Hogg had a rich inheritance. His shorter tales of wizardry and diablerie *are collected in* The Shepherd's Calendar. *That of* George Dobson's Expedition to Hell *is among them and is one of the best.*

There is no phenomenon in nature less understood, and about which greater nonsense is written than dreaming. It is a strange thing. For my part I do not understand it, nor have I any desire to do so; and I firmly believe that no philosopher that ever wrote knows a particle more about it than I do, however elaborate and subtle the theories he may advance concerning it. He knows not even what sleep is, nor can he define its nature, so as to enable any common mind to comprehend him; and how, then, can he define that ethereal part of it, wherein the soul holds intercourse with the external world? — how, in that state of abstraction, some ideas force themselves upon us, in spite of all our efforts to get rid of them; while others, which we have resolved to bear about with us by night as well as by day, refuse us their fellowship, even at periods when we most require their aid?

No, no; the philosopher knows nothing about either; and if he says he does, I entreat you not to believe him. He does not know what mind is; even his own mind, to which one would think he has the most direct access: far less can he estimate the operations and powers of that of any other intelligent being. He does not even know with all his subtlety, whether it be a power distinct from his body, or essentially the same, and only incidentally and temporarily endowed with different qualities. He sets himself to discover at what period of his existence the union was established. He is baffled; for Consciousness refuses the intelligence, declaring, that she cannot carry him far enough back to ascertain it. He tries to discover the precise moment when it is dissolved, but on this Consciousness is altogether silent; and all is darkness and mystery; for the origin, the manner of continuance, and the time and mode of breaking up of the union between soul and body, are in reality undiscoverable

19

by our natural faculties — are not patent, beyond the possibility of mistake; but whosoever can read his Bible, and solve a dream, can do either, without being subjected to any material error. It is on this ground that I like to contemplate, not the theory of dreams, but the dreams themselves; because they prove to the unlettered man, in a very forcible manner, a distinct existence of the soul, and its lively and rapid intelligence with external nature, as well as with a world of spirits with which it has no acquaintance, when the body is lying dormant, and the same to the soul as if sleeping in death.

I account nothing of any dream that relates to the actions of the day; the person is not sound asleep who dreams about these things; there is no division between matter and mind, but they are mingled together in a sort of chaos — what a farmer would call compost — fermenting and disturbing one another. I find that in all dreams of that kind, men of every profession have dreams peculiar to their own occupations; and, in the country, at least, their import is generally understood. Every man's body is a barometer. A thing made up of the elements must be affected by their various changes and convulsions; and so the body assuredly is. When I was a shepherd, and all the comforts of my life depended so much on good or bad weather, the first thing I did every morning was strictly to overhaul the dreams of the night; and I found that I could calculate better from them than from the appearance and changes of the sky. I know a keen sportsman who pretends that his dreams never deceive him. If he dream of angling, or pursuing salmon in deep waters, he is sure of rain; but if fishing on dry ground, or in waters so low that the fish cannot get from him, it forebodes drought; hunting or shooting hares is snow, and moorfowl wind, &c. But the most extraordinary professional dream on record is, without all doubt, that well-known one of George Dobson, coach-driver in Edinburgh, which I shall here relate; for though it did not happen in the shepherd's cot, it has often been recited there.

George was part proprietor and driver of a hackney-coach in Edinburgh, when such vehicles were scarce; and one day a gentleman, whom he knew, came to him and said:

— "George, you must drive me and my son here out to —," a certain place that he named, somewhere in the vicinity of Edinburgh.

"Sir," said George, "I never heard tell of such a place, and I cannot drive you to it unless you give me very particular directions."

"It is false," returned the gentleman, "there is no man in Scotland who knows the road to that place better than you do. You have never driven on any other road all your life; and I insist on you taking us."

"Very well, sir," said George, "I'll drive you to hell, if you have a mind; only you are to direct me on the road."

"Mount and drive on, then," said the other, "and no fear of the road."

George did so, and never in his life did he see his horses go at such a noble rate; they snorted, they pranced, and they flew on; and as the whole road appeared to lie down-hill, he deemed that he should soon come to his journey's end. Still he drove on at the same rate, far, far down-hill, — and so fine an open road he never travelled, — till by degrees it grew so dark that he could not see to drive any farther. He called to the gentleman, inquiring what he should do; who answered that this was the place they were bound to, so he might draw up, dismiss them, and return. He did so, alighted from the dickie, wondered at his foaming horses, and forthwith opened the coach-door, held the rim of his hat with the one hand, and with the other demanded his fare.

"You have driven us in fine style, George," said the elder gentleman, "and deserve to be remembered; but it is needless for us to settle just now, as you must meet us here again to-morrow precisely at twelve o'clock."

"Very well, sir," said George; "there is likewise an old account, you know, and some toll-money;" which indeed there was.

"It shall be all settled to-morrow, George, and moreover, I fear there will be some toll-money to-day."

"I perceived no tolls to-day, your honour," said George.

"But I perceived one, and not very far back neither, which I suspect you will have difficulty in repassing without a regular ticket. What a pity I have no change on me!"

21

"I never saw it otherwise with your honour," said George, jocularly; "what a pity it is you should always suffer yourself to run short of change!"

"I will give you that which is as good, George," said the gentleman; and he gave him a ticket written with red ink, which the honest coachman could not read. He, however, put it into his sleeve, and inquired of his employer where that same toll was which he had not observed, and how it was that they did not ask toll from him as he came through? The gentleman replied, by informing George that there was no road out of that domain, and that whoever entered it, must either remain in it, or return by the same path; so they never asked any toll till the person's return, when they were at times highly capricious; but that the ticket he had given him would answer his turn. And he then asked George if he did not perceive a gate, with a number of men in black standing about it.

"Oho! Is yon the spot?" says George; "then, I assure your honour, yon is no toll-gate, but a private entrance into a great man's mansion; for do not I know two or three of the persons yonder to be gentlemen of the law, whom I have driven often and often? and as good fellows they are too as any I know — men who never let themselves run short of change! Good day. — Twelve o'clock to-morrow?"

"Yes, twelve o'clock noon, precisely;" and with that, George's employer vanished in the gloom, and left him to wind his way out of that dreary labyrinth the best way he could. He found it no easy matter, for his lamps were not lighted, and he could not see an ell before him — he could not even perceive his horses' ears; and what was worse, there was a rushing sound, like that of a town on fire, all around him, that stunned his senses, so that he could not tell whether his horses were moving or standing still. George was in the greatest distress imaginable, and was glad when he perceived the gate before him, with his two identical friends, men of the law, still standing. George drove boldly up, accosted them by their names, and asked what they were doing there; they made him no answer, but pointed to the gate and the keeper. George was terrified to look at this latter personage, who now came up and seized his horses by

22

"Out of this gate you pass no more"

the reins, refusing to let him pass. In order to introduce himself, in some degree, to this austere toll-man, George asked him, in a jocular manner, how he came to employ his two eminent friends as assistant gate-keepers?

"Because they are among the last comers," replied the ruffian, churlishly. "You will be an assistant here to-morrow."

"The devil I will sir."

"Yes, the devil you will, sir."

"I'll be d — d if I do, then — that I will!"

"Yes, you'll be d — d if you do — that you will."

"Let my horses go in the mean time, then, sir, that I may proceed to my journey."

"Nay."

"Nay! — Dare you say nay to me, sir? My name is George Dobson, of the Pleasance, Edinburgh, coach-driver, and coach-proprietor, too; and no man shall say *nay* to me, as long as I can pay my way. I have his Majesty's license, and I'll go and come as I choose — and that I will. Let go my horses there, and tell me what is your demand."

"Well, then, I'll let your horses go," said the keeper, "but I'll keep yourself for a pledge." And with that he let go the horses, and seized honest George by the throat, who struggled in vain to disengage himself, and swore, and threatened, according to his own confession, most bloodily. His horses flew off like the wind, so swift that the coach seemed flying in the air, and scarcely bounding on the earth once in a quarter of a mile. George was in furious wrath, for he saw that his grand coach and harness would all be broken to pieces, and his gallant pair of horses maimed or destroyed; and how was his family's bread now to be won!
— He struggled, threatened, and prayed in vain; — the intolerable toll-man was deaf to all remonstrances. He once more appealed to his two genteel acquaintances of the law, reminding them how he had of late driven them to Roslin on a Sunday, along with two ladies, who, he supposed, were their sisters, from their familiarity, when not another coachman in town would engage with them. But the gentlemen, very ungenerously, only shook their heads, and pointed to the gate. George's circumstances now became

24

desperate, and again he asked the hideous tollman what right he had to detain him, and what were his charges.

"What right have I to detain you, sir, say you? Who are you that make such a demand here? Do you know where you are, sir?"

"No, faith, I do not," returned George; I wish I did. But I *shall* know, and make you repent your insolence, too. My name, I told you, is George Dobson, licensed coach-hirer in Pleasance, Edinburgh; and to get full redress of you for this unlawful interruption, I only desire to know where I am."

"Then, sir, if it can give you so much satisfaction to know where you are," said the keeper, with a malicious grin, "you *shall* know, and you may take instruments by the hands of your two friends there, instituting a legal prosecution. Your address, you may be assured, will be most ample, when I inform you that you are in HELL! and out of this gate you pass no more."

This was rather a damper to George, and he began to perceive that nothing would be gained in such a place by the strong hand, so he addressed the inexorable toll-man, whom he now dreaded more than ever, in the following terms: "But I must go home at all events, you know, sir, to unyoke my two horses, and put them up, and to inform Christy Halliday, my wife, of my engagement. And, bless me! I never recollected till this moment, that I am engaged to be back here to-morrow at twelve o'clock, and see, here is a free ticket for my passage this way."

The keeper took the ticket with one hand, but still held George with the other. "Oho! were you in with our honourable friend, Mr. R — of L — y?" said he. "He has been on our books for a long while; — however, this will do, only you must put your name to it likewise; and the engagement is this — You, by this instrument, engage your soul, that you will return here by to-morrow at noon."

"Catch me there, billy!" say George. "I'll engage no such thing, depend on it; — that I will not."

"Then remain where you are," said the keeper, "for there is no other alternative. We like best for people to come here in their own way, — in the way of their business;" and with that he flung George backwards, heels-over-head down hill, and closed the gate.

George finding all remonstrance vain, and being desirous once more to see the open day, and breathe the fresh air, and likewise to see Christy Halliday, his wife, and set his house and stable in some order, came up again, and in utter desperation, signed the bond, and was suffered to depart. He then bounded away on the track of his horses, with more than ordinary swiftness, in hopes to overtake them; and always now and then uttered a loud Wo! in hopes that they might hear and obey, though he could not come in sight of them. But George's grief was but beginning; for at a well-known and dangerous spot, where there was a tan-yard on the one hand, and a quarry on the other, he came to his gallant steeds overturned, the coach smashed to pieces, Dawtie with two of her legs broken, and Duncan dead. This was more than the worthy coachman could bear, and many degrees worse than being in hell. There, his pride and manly spirit bore him up against the worst of treatment; but here his heart entirely failed him, and he laid himself down, with his face on his two hands, and wept bitterly, bewailing, in the most deplorable terms, his two gallant horses, Dawtie and Duncan.

While lying in this inconsolable state, some one took hold of his shoulder, and shook it; and a well-known voice said to him, "Geordie! what is the matter wi' ye, Geordie?" George was provoked beyond measure at the insolence of the question, for he knew the voice to be that of Kirsty Halliday, his wife. "I think you needna ask that, seeing what you see," said George. "O, my poor Dawtie, where are a' your jinkings and prancings now, your moopings and your wincings? I'll ne'er be a proud man again — bereaved o' my bonny pair!"

"Get up, George; get up, and bestir yourself," said Chirsty Halliday, his wife. "You are wanted directly, to bring in the Lord President in the Parliament House. It is a great storm, and he must be there by nine o'clock. — Get up — rouse yourself, and make ready — his servant is waiting for you."

"Woman, you are demented!" cried George. "How can I go and bring in the Lord President, when my coach is broken in pieces, my poor Dawtie lying with twa of her legs broken, and Duncan dead? And, moreover, I have a

26

previous engagement, for I am obliged to be in hell before twelve o'clock."

Chirsty Halliday now laughed outright, and continued long in a fit of laughter; but George never moved his head from the pillow, but lay and groaned, — for, in fact, he was all this while lying snug in his bed; while the tempest without was roaring with great violence, and which circumstance may perhaps account for the rushing and deafening sound which astounded him so much in hell. But so deeply was he impressed with the idea of the reality of his dream, that he would do nothing but lie and moan, persisting and believing in the truth of all he had seen. His wife now went and informed her neighbours of her husband's plight, and of his singular engagement with Mr. R — of L — y at twelve o'clock. She persuaded one friend to harness the horses, and go for the Lord President; but all the rest laughed immoderately at poor coachy's predicament. It was, however, no laughing to him; he never raised his head, and his wife becoming at last uneasy about the frenzied state of his mind, made him repeat every circumstance of his adventure to her (for he would never believe or admit that it was a dream), which he did in the terms above narrated; and she perceived or dreaded that he was becoming somewhat feverish. She went out, and told Dr. Wood of her husband's malady, and of his solemn engagement to be in hell at twelve o'clock.

"He maunna* keep it, dearie. He maunna keep that engagement at no rate," said Dr. Wood. "Set back the clock an hour or twa, to drive him past the time, and I'll ca' in the course of my rounds. Are ye sure he hasna been drinking hard?" — She assured him he had not. — "Weel, weel, ye maun tell him that he maunna keep that engagement at no rate. Set back the clock, and I'll come and see him. It is a frenzy that maunna be trifled with. Ye maunna laugh at it, dearie, — maunna laugh at it. Maybe a nervish fever, wha kens."

The Doctor and Chirsty left the house together, and as their road lay the same way for a space, she fell a-telling him

*maun, must; maunna, must not

27

of the two young lawyers whom George saw standing at the gate of hell, and whom the porter had described as two of the last comers. When the Doctor heard this, he stayed his hurried, stooping pace in one moment, turned full round on the woman, and fixing his eyes on her, that gleamed with a deep unstable lustre, he said. "What's that ye were saying dearie? What's that ye were saying? Repeat it again to me, every word." She did so. On which the Doctor held up his hands, as if palsied with astonishment, and uttered some fervent ejaculations. "I'll go with you straight," said he, "before I visit another patient. This is wonderfu'! it is terrible! The young gentlemen are both at rest — both lying corpses at this time! Fine young men — I attended them both — died of the same exterminating disease — Oh, this is wonderful; this is wonderful!"

The Doctor kept Chirsty half running all the way down the High Street and St. Mary's Wynd, at such a pace did he walk, never lifting his eyes from the pavement, but always exclaiming now and then, "It is wonderful! most wonderfu'!" At length, prompted by woman's natural curiosity, Chirsty inquired at the Doctor if he knew any thing of their friend Mr — of L — y. But he shook his head, and replied, "Na, na dearie, — ken naething about him. He and his son are baith in London, — ken naething about him; but the tither† is awfu' — it is perfectly awfu'!"

When Dr. Wood reached his patient he found him very low, but only a little feverish; so he made all haste to wash his head with vinegar and cold water, and then he covered the crown with a treacle plaster, and made the same application to the soles of his feet, awaiting the issue. George revived a little, when the Doctor tried to cheer him up by joking him about his dream; but on mention of that he groaned, and shook his head. "So you are convinced, dearie, that it is nae dream?" said the Doctor.

"Dear sir, how could it be a dream?" said the patient. "I was there in person, with Mr. R — and his son; and see, here are the marks of the porter's fingers on my throat." — Dr. Wood looked, and distinctly saw two or three red spots on

†*tither*, the other

one side of his throat, which confounded him not a little. — "I assure you, sir," continued George, "it was no dream, which I know to my sad experience. I have lost my coach and horses, — and what more have I? — signed the bond with my own hand, and in person entered into the most solemn and terrible engagement."

"But ye're no to keep it, I tell ye," said Dr. Wood; "ye're no to keep it at no rate. It is a sin to enter into a compact wi' the deil, but it is a far greater ane to keep it. Sae let Mr. R — and his son bide where they are yonder, for ye sanna stir a foot to bring them out the day."

"Oh, oh, Doctor!" groaned the poor fellow, "this is not a thing to be made a jest o'! I feel that it is an engagement that I cannot break. Go I must, and that very shortly. Yes, yes, go I must, and go I will, although I should borrow David Barclay's pair." With that he turned his face towards the wall, groaned deeply, and fell into a lethargy, while Dr. Wood caused them to let him alone, thinking if he would sleep out the appointed time, which was at hand, he would be safe; but all the time he kept feeling his pulse, and by degrees showed symptons of uneasiness. His wife ran for a clergyman of famed abilities, to pray and converse with her husband, in hopes by the means to bring him to his senses; but after his arrival, George never spoke more, save calling to his horses, as if encouraging them to run with great speed; and thus in imagination driving at full career to keep his appointment, he went off in a paroxysm, after a terrible struggle, precisely within a few minutes of twelve o'clock.

A circumstance not known at the time of George's death this singular professional dream the more remarkable and unique in all its parts. It was a terrible storm on the night of the dream, as has been already mentioned, and during the time of the hurricane, a London smack went down off Wearmouth about three in the morning. Among the sufferers were the Hon. Mr. R — of L — y, and his son! George could not know aught of this at break of day, for it was not known in Scotland till the day of his interment; and as little knew he of the deaths of the two young lawyers, who both died of the small-pox the evening before.

Robert Louis Stevenson (1850-94) was a native of Edinburgh city. Though not a Borderer, he has something in common with Scott and Hogg. Like Scott he wrote tales of adventure and romantic history, and was fascinated by apparitions. He was fascinated still more by the conflict between good and evil in one personality, a theme which had already appeared in Hogg's Confessions of a Justified Sinner. *(In one of Stevenson's most famous books,* Dr Jekyll and Mr Hyde, *the duality is not so much of good and evil as of respectability in Jekyll and utter wickedness in Hyde; the latter is stronger.)*

Stevenson does not accompany Scott and Hogg in their other adventures — into Elfhame. He knew no elves or fairies, only the darker figures of witches and wizards (his Thrawn Janet *is a superb example, and so is* Tod Lapraik *in* Catriona) *and 'Auld Hornie', the devil himself in one form or other.*

MARKHEIM

"Yes," said the dealer, "our windfalls are of various kinds. Some customers are ignorant, and then I touch a dividend on my superior knowledge. Some are dishonest," and here he held up the candle, so that the light fell strongly on his visitor, "and in that case," he continued, "I profit by my virtue."

Markheim had but just entered from the daylight streets, and his eyes had not yet grown familiar with the mingled shine and darkness in the shop. At these pointed words, and before the near presence of the flame, he blinked painfully and looked aside.

The dealer chuckled. "You come to me on Christmas Day," he resumed, "when you know that I am alone in my house, put up my shutters, and make a point of refusing business. Well, you will have to pay for that; you will have to pay for my loss of time, when I should be balancing my books; you will have to pay besides, for a kind of manner that I remark in you to-day very strongly. I am the essence of discretion, and ask no awkward questions: but when a customer cannot look me in the eye, he has to pay for it." The dealer once more chuckled; and then, changing to his usual business voice, though still with a note of irony, "You can give, as usual, a clear account of how you came into the possession of the object?" he continued. "Still your uncle's cabinet? A remarkable collector, sir!"

And the little pale, round-shouldered dealer stood almost on tip-toe, looking over the top of his gold spectacles, and nodding his head with every mark of disbelief. Markheim returned his gaze with one of infinite pity, and a touch of horror.

"This time," said he, "you are in error. I have not come to sell, but to buy. I have no curios to dispose of; my uncle's cabinet is bare to the wainscot; even were it still intact, I have done well on the Stock Exchange, and should more likely add to it than otherwise, and my errand to-day is simplicity itself. I seek a Christmas present for a lady," he continued, waxing more fluent as he struck into the speech he had prepared; "and certainly I owe you every excuse for thus disturbing you upon so small a matter. But the thing was neglected yesterday; I must produce my little compliment at dinner; and, as you very well know, a rich marriage is not a thing to be neglected."

There followed a pause, during which the dealer seemed to weigh this statement incredulously. The ticking of many clocks among the curious lumber of the shop, and the faint rushing of the cabs in a near thoroughfare, filled up the interval of silence.

"Well, sir," said the dealer, "be it so. You are an old customer after all; and if, as you say, you have the chance of a good marriage, far be it from me to be an obstacle. Here is a nice thing for a lady now," he went on, "this hand glass — fifteenth century, warranted; comes from a good collection, too; but I reserve the name, in the interests of my customer, who was just like yourself, my dear sir, the nephew and sole heir of a remarkable collector."

The dealer, while he thus ran on in his dry and biting voice, had stooped to take the object from its place; and, as he had done so, a shock had passed through Markheim, a start both of hand and foot, a sudden leap of many tumultuous passions to the face. It passed as swiftly as it came, and left no trace beyond a certain trembling of the hand that now received the glass.

"A glass," he said hoarsely, and then paused, and repeated it more clearly. "A glass? For Christmas? Surely not?"

"And why not?" cried the dealer. "Why not a glass?"

Markheim was looking upon him with an indefinable expression. "You ask me why not?" he said. "Why, look here — look in it — look at yourself! Do you like to see it? No! nor I — nor any man."

The little man had jumped back when Markheim had so suddenly confronted him with the mirror; but now, perceiving there was nothing worse on hand, he chuckled. "Your future lady, sir, must be pretty hard favoured," said he.

"I ask you," said Markheim, "for a Christmas present, and you give me this — this damned reminder of years, and sins and follies — this hand-conscience! Did you mean it? Had you a thought in your mind? Tell me. It will be better for you if you do. Come, tell me about yourself. I hazard a guess now, that you are in secret a very charitable man?"

The dealer looked closely at his companion. It was very odd, Markheim did not appear to be laughing; there was something in his face like an eager sparkle of hope, but nothing of mirth.

"What are you driving at?" the dealer asked.

"Not charitable?" returned the other gloomily. "Not charitable; not pious; not scrupulous; unloving, unbeloved; a hand to get money, a safe to keep it. Is that all? Dear God, man, is that all?"

"I will tell you what it is," began the dealer, with some sharpness, and then broke off again into a chuckle. "But I see this is a love match of yours, and you have been drinking the lady's health."

"Ah!" cried Markheim, with a strange curiosity. "Ah, have you been in love? Tell me about that."

"I," cried the dealer. "I in love! I never had the time, or have I the time to-day for all this nonsense. Will you take the glass?"

"Where is the hurry?" returned Markheim. "It is very pleasant to stand here talking; and life is so short and insecure that I would not hurry away from any pleasure — no, not even from so mild a one as this. We should rather cling, cling to what little we can get, like a man at a cliff's edge. Every second is a cliff, if you think upon it — a cliff a mile high — high enough, if we fall, to dash us out of every feature of humanity. Hence it is best to talk pleasantly. Let us talk of each other; why should we wear this mask? Let us be confidential. Who knows, we might become friends?"

"I have just one word to say to you," said the dealer. "Either make your purchase, or walk out of my shop!"

"True, true," said Markheim. "Enough fooling. To business. Show me something else."

The dealer stooped once more, this time to replace the glass upon the shelf, his thin blond hair falling over his eyes as he did so. Markheim moved a little nearer, with one hand in the pocket of his greatcoat; he drew himself up and filled his lungs; at the same time many different emotions were depicted together on his face — terror, horror, and resolve, fascination and a physical repulsion; and through a haggard lift of his upper lip, his teeth looked out.

"This, perhaps, may suit," observed the dealer: and then, as he began to re-arise, Markheim bounded from behind upon his victim. The long, skewerlike dagger flashed and fell. The dealer struggled like a hen, striking his temple on the shelf, and then tumbled on the floor in a heap.

Time had some score of small voices in that shop, some stately and slow as was becoming to their great age; others garrulous and hurried. All these told out the seconds in an intricate chorus of tickings. Then the passage of a lad's feet, heavily running on the pavement, broke in upon these smaller voices and startled Markheim into the consciousness of his surroundings. He looked about him awfully. The candle stood on the counter, its flame solemnly wagging in a draught; and by that inconsiderable movement, the whole room was filled with noiseless bustle and kept heaving like a sea: the tall shadows nodding, the gross blots of darkness swelling and dwindling as with respiration, the faces of the portraits and the china gods

33

changing and wavering like images in water. The inner door stood ajar, and peered into that leaguer of shadows with a long slit of daylight like a pointing finger.

From these fear-stricken rovings, Markheim's eyes returned to the body of his victim, where it lay both humped and sprawling, incredibly small and strangely meaner than in life. In these poor, miserly clothes, in that ungainly attitude, the dealer lay like so much sawdust. Markheim had feared to see it, and, lo! it was nothing. And yet, as he gazed, this bundle of old clothes and pool of blood began to find eloquent voices. There it must lie; there was none to work the cunning hinges or direct the miracle of locomotion — there it must lie till it was found. Found! ay, and then? Then would this dead flesh lift up a cry that would ring over England, and fill the world with the echoes of pursuit. Ay, dead or not, this was still the enemy. "Time was that when the brains were out," he thought; and the first word struck into his mind. Time, now that the deed was accomplished — time, which had closed for the victim, had become instant and momentous for the slayer.

The thought was yet in his mind, when, first one and then another, with every variety of pace and voice — one deep as the bell from a cathedral turret, another ringing on its treble notes the prelude of a waltz — the clocks began to strike the hour of three in the afternoon.

The sudden outbreak of so many tongues in that dumb chamber staggered him. He began to bestir himself, going to and fro with the candle, beleaguered by moving shadows, and startled to the soul by chance reflections. In many rich mirrors, some of home design, some from Venice or Amsterdam, he saw his face repeated and repeated, as it were an army of spies; his own eyes met and detected him, and the sound of his own steps, lightly as they fell, vexed the surrounding quiet. And still, as he continued to fill his pockets, his mind accused him with a sickening iteration, of the thousand faults of his design. He should have chosen a more quiet hour; he should have prepared an alibi; he should not have used a knife; he should have been more cautious, and only bound and gagged the dealer, and not killed him; he should have been more bold, and killed the servant also; he should have done all things otherwise; poignant regrets, weary, incessant toiling of the mind to change what was unchangeable, to plan what was now useless, to be the architect of the irrevocable past. Meanwhile, and behind all this activity, brute terrors, like the scurrying of rats in a deserted attic, filled the more remote chambers of his brain with riot; the hand of the constable would fall heavy on his shoulder, and his nerves would jerk like a hooked fish; or he beheld, in galloping defile, the dock, the prison, the gallows, and the black coffin.

Terror of the people in the street sat down before his mind like a besieging army. It was impossible, he thought, but that some rumour of the struggle must have reached their ears and set on edge their curiosity; and now, in all the neighbouring houses, he divined them sitting motionless and with uplifted ear — solitary people, condemned to spend Christmas dwelling alone on memories of the past, and now startingly recalled from that tender exercise; happy family parties, struck into silence round the table, the mother still with raised finger: every degree and age and humour, but all, by their own hearths, prying and hearkening and weaving the rope that was to hang him. Sometimes it seemed to him he could not move too softly; the clink of the tall Bohemian goblets rang out loudly like a bell; and alarmed by the bigness of the ticking, he was tempted to stop the clocks. And then, again, with a swift transition of his terrors, the very silence of the place appeared a source of peril, and a thing to strike and freeze the passer-by; and he would step more boldly, and bustle aloud among the contents of the shops, and imitate, with elaborate bravado, the movements of a busy man at ease in his own house.

But he was now so pulled about by different alarms that, while one portion of his mind was still alert and cunning, another trembled on the brink of lunacy. One hallucination in particular took a strong hold on his credulity. The neighbour hearkening with white face beside his window, the passer-by arrested by a horrible surmise on the pavement — these could at worse suspect, they could not know; through the brick walls and shuttered windows only sounds could penetrate. But here, within the house, was he alone? He knew he was; he had watched the servant set forth sweet-hearting, in her poor best, "out for the day" written in every ribbon and smile. Yes, he was alone, of course; and yet, in the bulk of empty house above him, he could surely hear a stir of delicate footing he was surely conscious, inexplicably conscious of some presence. Ay, surely; to every room and corner of the house his imagination followed it; and now it was a faceless thing, and yet had eyes to see with; and again it was a shadow of himself; and yet again behold the image of the dead dealer, reinspired with cunning and hatred.

At times, with a strong effort, he would glance at the open door which still seemed to repel his eyes. The house was tall, the skylight small and dirty, the day blind with fog; and the light that filtered down to the ground story was exceedingly faint, and showed dimly on the threshold of the shop. And yet, in that strip of doubtful brightness, did there not hang wavering a shadow?

Suddenly, from the street outside, a very jovial gentleman began to beat with a staff on the shop-door, accompanying his blows with shouts and railleries in which the dealer was continually called upon by name. Markheim, smitten into ice, glanced at the dead man. But no! he lay quite still; he was fled away far beyond earshot of these blows and shoutings; he was sunk beneath seas of silence; and his name, which would once have caught his notice above the howling of a storm, had become an empty sound. And presently the jovial gentleman desisted from his knocking and departed.

Here was a broad hint to hurry what remained to be done, to get forth from this accusing neighbourhood, to plunge into a bath of London multitudes, and to reach, on the other side of day, that haven of safety and apparent innocence — his bed. One visitor had come: at any moment another might follow and be more obstinate. To have done the deed, and yet not to reap the profit, would be too abhorrent a failure. The money, that was now Markheim's concern; and as a means to that, the keys.

He glanced over his shoulder at the open door, where the

shadow was still lingering and shivering; and with no conscious repugnance of the mind, yet with a tremor of the belly, he drew near the body of his victim. The human character had quite departed. Like a suit half-stuffed with bran, the limbs lay scattered, the trunk doubled, on the floor; and yet the thing repelled him. Although so dingy and inconsiderable to the eye, he feared it might have more significance to the touch. He took the body by the shoulders, and turned it on its back. It was strangely light and supple, and the limbs, as if they had been broken, fell into the oddest postures. The face was robbed of all expression; but it was as pale as wax, and shockingly smeared with blood about one temple. That was, for Markheim, the one displeasing circumstance. It carried him back, upon the instant, to a certain fair-day in a fishers' village: a gray day, a piping wind, a crowd upon the street, the blare of brasses, and booming of drums, the nasal voice of a ballad singer; and a boy going to and fro, buried over head in the crowd and divided between interest and fear, until, coming out upon the chief place of concourse, he beheld a booth and a great screen with pictures, dismally designed, garishly coloured: Brownrigg with her apprentice; the Mannings with their murdered guest; Weare in the death-grip of Thurtell; and a score besides of famous crimes. The thing was as clear as an illusion; he was once again that little boy; he was looking once again, and with the same sense of physical revolt, at these vile pictures; he was still stunned by the thumping of the drums. A bar of that day's music returned upon his memory; and at that, for the first time, a qualm came over him, a breath of nausea, a sudden weakness of the joints, which he must instantly resist and conquer.

He judged it more prudent to confront than to flee from these considerations; looking the more hardily in the dead face, bending his mind to realise the nature and greatness of his crime. So little a while ago that face had moved with every change of sentiment, that pale mouth had spoken, that body had been all on fire with governable energies; and now, and by his act, that piece of life had been arrested, as the horologist, with interjected finger, arrests the beating of the clock. So he reasoned in vain; he could rise to no more

37

remorseful consciousness; the same heart which had shuddered before the painted effigies of crime, looked on its reality unmoved. At best, he felt a gleam of pity for one who had been endowed in vain with all those faculties that can make the world a garden of enchantment, one who had never lived and who was now dead. But of penitence, no, not a tremor.

With that, shaking himself clear of these considerations, he found the keys and advanced towards the open door of the shop. Outside, it had begun to rain smartly; and the sound of the shower upon the roof had banished silence. Like some dripping cavern, the chambers of the house were haunted by an incessant echoing, which filled the ear and mingled with the ticking of the clocks. And, as Markheim approached the door, he seemed to hear, in answer to his own cautious tread, the steps of another foot withdrawing up the stair. The shadow still palpitated loosely on the threshold. He threw a ton's weight of resolve upon his muscles, and drew back the door.

The faint, foggy daylight glimmered dimly on the bare floor and stairs; on the bright suit of armour posted, halbert in hand, upon the landing; and on the dark wood-carvings, and framed pictures that hung against the yellow panels of the wainscot. So loud was the beating of the rain through all the house that, in Markheim's ears, it began to be distinguished into many different sounds. Footsteps and sighs, the tread of regiments marching in the distance, the chink of money in the counting, and the creaking of doors held stealthily ajar, appeared to mingle with the patter of the drops upon the cupola and the gushing of the water in the pipes. The sense that he was not alone grew upon him to the verge of madness. On every side he was haunted and begirt by presences. He heard them moving in the upper chambers; from the shop, he heard the dead man getting to his legs; and as he began with a great effort to mount the stairs, feet fled quietly before him and followed stealthily behind. If he were but deaf, he thought, how tranquilly he would possess his soul! And then again, and hearkening with ever fresh attention, he blessed himself for that unresting sense which held the outposts and stood a trusty sentinel upon his life.

His head turned continually on his neck; his eyes, which seemed starting from their orbits, scouted on every side, and on every side were half-rewarded as with the tail of something nameless vanishing. The four-and-twenty steps to the first floor were four-and-twenty agonies.

On that first storey, the doors stood ajar, three of them like three ambushes, shaking his nerves like the throats of cannon. He could never again, he felt, be sufficiently immured and fortified from men's observing eyes; he longed to be home, girt in by walls, buried among bedclothes, and invisible to all but God. And at that thought he wondered a little, recollecting tales of other murderers and the fear they were said to entertain of heavenly avengers. It was not so, at least, with him. He feared the laws of nature, lest, in their callous and immutable procedure, they should preserve some damning evidence of his crime. He feared tenfold more, with a slavish, superstitious terror, some scission in the continuity of man's experience, some wilful illegality of nature. He played a game of skill, depending on the rules, calculating consequence from cause; and what if nature, as the defeated tyrant overthrew the chess-board, should break the mould of their succession? The like had befallen Napoleon (so writers said) when the winter changed the time of its appearance. The like might befall Markheim: the solid walls might become transparent and reveal his doings like those of bees in a glass hive; the stout planks might yield under his foot like quicksands and detain him in their clutch; ay, and there were soberer accidents that might destroy him: if, for instance, the house should fall and imprison him, beside the body of his victim; or the house next door should fly on fire, and the firemen invade him from all sides. These things he feared; and, in a sense, these things might be called the hands of God reached forth against sin. But about God Himself he was at ease; his act was doubtless exceptional, but so were his excuses, which God knew; it was there, and not among men, that he felt sure of justice.

When he had got safe into the drawing-room, and shut the door behind him, he was aware of a respite from alarms. The room was quite dismantled, uncarpeted besides, and strewn with packing cases and incongruous furniture; several great pier-glasses, in which he beheld himself at various angles, like an actor on a stage; many pictures, framed and unframed, standing, with their faces to the wall; a fine Sheraton sideboard, a cabinet of marquetry, and a great old bed, with tapestry hangings. The windows opened to the floor; but by great good fortune the lower part of the shutters had been closed, and this concealed him from the neighbours. Here, then, Markheim drew in a packing case before the cabinet, and began to search among the keys. It was a long business, for there were many; and it was irksome, besides; for, after all, there might be nothing in the cabinet, and time was on the wing. But the closeness of the occupation sobered him. With the tail of his eye he saw the door — even glanced at it from time to time directly, like a besieged commander pleased to verify the good estate of his defences. But in truth he was at peace. The rain falling in the street sounded natural and pleasant. Presently on the other side, the notes of a piano were wakened to the music of a hymn, and the voices of many children took up the air and words. How stately, how comfortable was the melody! How fresh the youthful voices! Markheim gave ear to it smilingly, as he sorted out the keys; and his mind was thronged with answerable ideas and images; church-going children and the pealing of the high organ; children afield, bathers by the brookside, ramblers on the brambly common, kite-flyers in the windy and cloud-navigated sky; and then, at another cadence of the hymn, back again to church, and the somnolence of summer Sundays, and the high genteel voice of the parson (which he smiled a little to recall) and the painted Jacobean tombs, and the dim lettering of the Ten Commandments in the chancel.

And as he sat thus, at once busy and absent, he was startled to his feet. A flash of ice, a flash of fire, a bursting gush of blood, went over him, and then he stood transfixed and thrilling. A step mounted the stair slowly and steadily, and presently a hand was laid upon the knob, and the lock clicked, and the door opened.

Fear held Markheim in a vice. What to expect he knew not, whether the dead man walking, or the official ministers of human justice, or some chance witness blindly stumbling

Fear held Markheim in a vice

in to consign him to the gallows. But when a face was thrust into the aperture, glanced round the room, looked at him, nodded and smiled as if in friendly recognition, and then withdrew again, and the door closed behind it, his fear broke loose from his control in a hoarse cry. At the sound of this the visitant returned.

"Did you call me?" he asked pleasantly, and with that he entered the room and closed the door behind him.

Markheim stood and gazed at him with all his eyes. Perhaps there was a film upon his sight, but the outlines of the new-comer seemed to change and waver like those of the idols in the wavering candlelight of the shop; and at times he thought he knew him; and at times he thought he bore a likeness to himself; and always, like a lump of living terror, there lay in his bosom the conviction that this thing was not of the earth and not of God.

And yet the creature had a strange air of the commonplace, as he stood looking on Markheim with a smile; and when he added: "You are looking for the money, I believe?" it was in the tones of everyday politeness.

Markheim made no answer.

"I should warn you," resumed the other, "that the maid has left her sweetheart earlier than usual and will soon be here. If Mr. Markheim be found in this house, I need not describe to him the consequences."

"You know me?" cried the murderer. The visitor smiled. "You have long been a favourite of mine," he said; "and I have long observed and often sought to help you."

"What are you?" cried Markheim: "the devil?"

"What I may be," returned the other, "cannot affect the service I propose to render you."

"It can," cried Markheim; "it does! Be helped by you? No, never; not by you! You do not know me yet; thank God, you do not know me!"

"I know you," replied the visitant, with a sort of kind severity or rather firmness. "I know you to the soul."

"Know me!" cried Markheim. "Who can do so? My life is but a travesty and slander on myself. I have lived to belie my nature. All men do; all men are better than this disguise that grows about and stifles them. You see each dragged away by life, like one whom bravos have seized and muffled in a cloak. If they had their own control — if you could see their faces, they would be altogether different, they would shine out for heroes and saints! I am worse than most; myself is more overlaid; my excuse is known to me and God. But, had I the time, I could disclose myself."

"To me?" inquired the visitant.

"To you before all," returned the murderer. "I suppose you were intelligent. I thought — since you exist — you would prove a reader of the heart. And yet you would propose to judge me by my acts! Think of it; my acts! I was born and I have lived in a land of giants; giants have dragged me by the wrists since I was born out of my mother — the giants of circumstance. And you would judge me by my acts! But can you not look within? Can you not understand that evil is hateful to me? Can you not see within me the clear writing of conscience, never blurred by any wilful sophistry, although too often disregarded? Can you not read me for a thing that surely must be common as humanity — the unwilling sinner?"

"All this is very feelingly expressed," was the reply, " but it regards me not. These points of consistency are beyond my province, and I care not in the least by what compulsion you may have been dragged away, so as you are but carried in the right direction. But time flies; the servant delays, looking in the faces of the crowd and at the pictures on the hoardings, but still she keeps moving nearer; and remember, it is as if the gallows itself was striding towards you through the Christmas streets! Shall I help you; I, who know all? Shall I tell you where to find the money?"

"For what price?" asked Markheim.

"I offer you the service for a Christmas gift," returned the other.

Markheim could not refrain from smiling with a kind of bitter triumph. "No," said he, "I will take nothing at your hands; if I were dying of thirst, and it was your hand that put the pitcher to my lips, I should find the courage to refuse. It may be credulous, but I will do nothing to commit myself to evil."

"I have no objection to a deathbed repentance," observed

the visitant.

"Because you disbelieve their efficacy!" Markheim cried.

"I do not say so," returned the other; "but I look on these things from a different side, and when the life is done my interest falls. The man has lived to save me, to spread black looks under colour of religion, or to sow tares in the wheat-field, as you do, in a course of weak compliance with desire. Now that he draws so near to his deliverance, he can add but one act of service — to repent, to die smiling, and thus to build up in confidence and hope the more timorous of my surviving followers. I am not so hard a master. Try me. Accept my help. Please yourself in life as you have done hitherto; please yourself more amply, spread your elbow at the board; and when the night begins to fall and the curtains to be drawn, I tell you, for your greater comfort, that you will find it even easy to compound your quarrel with your conscience, and to make a truckling peace with God. I came but now from such a deathbed, and, the room was full of sincere mourners, listening to the man's last words: and when I looked into that face, which had been set as a flint against mercy, I found it smiling with hope."

"And do you, then suppose me such a creature?" asked Markheim. "Do you think I have no more generous aspirations than to sin, and sin, and sin, and, at the last, sneak into heaven? My heart rises at the thought. Is this, then, your experience of mankind? or is it because you find me with red hands that you presume such baseness? and is this crime of murder indeed so impious as to dry up the very springs of good?"

"Murder is to me no special category," replied the other. "All sins are murder, even as all life is war. I behold your race, like starving mariners on a raft, plucking crusts out of the hands of famine and feeding on each other's lives. I follow sins beyond the moment of their acting; I find in all that the last consequence is death; and to my eyes, the pretty maid who thwarts her mother with such taking graces on a question of a ball, drips no less visibly with human gore than such a murderer as yourself. Do I say that I follow sins? I follow virtues also; they differ not by the thickness of a nail, they are both scythes for the reaping angel of Death. Evil, for which I live, consists not in action but in character. The bad man is dear to me; not the bad act, whose fruits, if we could follow them far enough down the hurtling cataract of the ages, might yet be found more blessed than those of the rarest virtues. And it is not because you have killed a dealer, but because you are Markheim, that I offer to forward your escape."

"I will lay my heart open to you," answered Markheim. "This crime on which you find me is my last. On my way to it I have learned many lessons; itself is a lesson, a momentous lesson. Hitherto I have been driven with revolt to what I would not; I was a bond-slave to poverty, driven and scourged. There are robust virtues that can stand in these temptations; mine was not so: I had a thirst of pleasure. But to-day, and out of this deed, I pluck both warning and riches — both the power and a fresh resolve to be myself. I become in all things a free actor in the world; I begin to see myself all changed, these hands the agents of good, this heart at peace. Something comes over me out of the past; something of what I have dreamed on Sabbath evenings to the sound of the church organ, of what I forecast when I shed tears over noble books, or talked, an innocent child, with my mother. There lies my life; I have wandered a few years, but now I see once more my city of destination."

"You are to use this money on the Stock Exchange, I think?" remarked the visitor; "and there, if I mistake not, you have already lost some thousands?"

"Ah," said Markheim, "but this time I have a sure thing."

"This time, again, you will lose," replied the visitor quietly.

"Ah, but I keep back the half!" cried Markheim.

"That also you will lose," said the other.

The sweat started upon Markheim's brow. "Well, then, what matter?" he exclaimed. "Say it be lost, say I am plunged again in poverty, shall one part of me, and that the worse, continue until the end to override the better? Evil and good run strong in me, haling me both ways. I do not love the one thing, I love all. I can conceive great deeds, renunciations, martyrdoms; and though I be fallen to such a crime as murder, pity is no stranger to my thoughts. I pity the poor; who knows their trials better than myself? I pity and help them; I prize love, I love honest laughter; there is no good thing nor true thing on earth but I love it from my heart. And are my vices only to direct my life, and my virtues to lie without effect, like some passive lumber of the mind? Not so; good, also, is a spring of acts."

But the visitant raised his finger. "For six-and-thirty years that you have been in this world," said he, "through many changes of fortune and varieties of humour, I have watched you steadily fall. Fifteen years ago you would have started at a theft. Three years back you would have blenched at the name of murder. Is there any crime, is there any cruelty or meanness, from which you still recoil? — five years from now I shall detect you in the fact! Downward, downwards, lies your way; nor can anything but death avail to stop you."

"It is true," Markheim said huskily, "I have in some degree complied with evil. But it is so with all: the very saints, in the mere exercise of living, grow less dainty, and take on the tone of their surroundings."

"I will propound to you one simple question," said the other; "and as you answer, I shall read to you your moral horoscope. You have grown in many things more lax; possibly you do right to be so; and at any account, it is the same with all men. But granting that, are you in any one particular, however trifling, more difficult to please with your own conduct, or do you go in all things with a looser rein?"

"In any one?" repeated Markheim, with an anguish of consideration. "No," he added, with despair, "in none! I have gone down in all."

"Then," said the visitor, "content yourself with what you are, for you will never change; and the words of your part on this stage are irrevocably written down."

Markheim stood for a long while silent, and indeed it was the visitor who first broke the silence. "That being so," he said, "shall I show you the money?"

"And grace?" cried Markheim.

"Have you not tried it?" returned the other. "Two or three years ago, did I not see you on the platform of revival meetings, and was not your voice the loudest in the hymn?"

"It is true," said Markheim; "and I see clearly what remains for me by way of duty. I thank you for these lessons from my soul; my eyes are opened, and I behold myself at last for what I am."

At this moment, the sharp note of the door-bell rang through the house; and the visitant, as though this were some concerted signal for which he had been waiting, changed at once in his demeanour.

"The maid!" he cried. "She has returned, as I forewarned you, and there is now before you one more difficult passage. Her master, you must say, is ill; you must let her in, with an assured but rather serious countenance — no smiles, no overacting, and I promise you success! Once the girl within, and the door closed, the same dexterity that has already rid you of the dealer will relieve you of this last danger in your path. Thenceforward you have the whole evening — the whole night, if needful — to ransack the treasures of the house and to make good your safety. This is help that comes to you with the mask of danger. Up!" he cried; "up, friend; your life hangs trembling in the scales: up, and act!"

Markheim steadily regarded his counsellor. "If I be condemned to evil acts" he said, "there is still one door to freedom open — I can cease from action. If my life be an ill thing, I can lay it down. Though I be, as you say truly, at the beck of every small temptation, I can yet, by one decisive gesture, place myself beyond the reach of all. My love of good is damned to barrenness; it may, and let it be! But I have still my hatred of evil; and from that, to your galling disappointment, you shall see that I can draw both energy and courage."

The features of the visitor began to undergo a wonderful and lovely change: they brightened and softened with a tender triumph, and, even as they brightened, faded and dislimned. But Markheim did not pause to watch or understand the transformation. He opened the door and went downstairs very slowly, thinking to himself. His past went soberly before him; he beheld it as it was, ugly and strenuous like a dream, random as chance-medley — a scene of defeat. Life, as he thus reviewed it, tempted him no longer; but on the farther side he perceived a quiet haven for his bark. He paused in the passage, and looked into the shop, where the candle still burned by the dead body. It was strangely silent. Thoughts of the dealer swarmed into his mind, as he stood gazing. And then the bell once more broke out into impatient clamour.

He confronted the maid upon the threshold with something like a smile.

"You had better go for the police," said he: "I have killed your master."

The legend or mystery of Glamis Castle in Angus, home of the Earls of Strathmore and Kinghorn, the family of the Queen Mother, has fascinated many minds and eluded most of them. Where is the secret chamber, and who inhabited it? Sir Walter Scott was aware of the spell when he visited Glamis; as he writes in his Letters on Demonology and Witchcraft:

I was only nineteen or twenty years old, when I happened to pass a night in the magnificent old baronial castle of Glammis, the hereditary seat of the Earls of Strathmore. The hoary pile contains much in its appearance, and in the traditions connected with it, impressive to the imagination. It was the scene of the murder of a Scottish king of great antiquity; not indeed the gracious Duncan, with whom the name naturally associates itself, but Malcolm the Second. It contains also a curious monument of the peril of feudal times, being a secret chamber, the entrance of which, by the law or custom of the family, must only be known to three persons at once, viz., the Earl of Strathmore, his heir apparent, and any third person whom they may take into their confidence. The extreme antiquity of the building is vouched by the immense thickness of the walls, and the wild and straggling arrangement of the accommodation within doors. As the late Earl of Strathmore seldom resided in that ancient mansion, it was, when I was there, but half-furnished, and that with movables of great antiquity, which,

48

with the pieces of chivalric armour hanging upon the walls, greatly contributed to the general effect of the whole. After a very hospitable reception from the late Peter Proctor, Esq., then seneschal of the castle, in Lord Strathmore's absence, I was conducted to my apartment in a distant corner of the building. I must own, that as I heard door after door shut, after my conductor had retired, I began to consider myself too far from the living and somewhat too near the dead. We had passed through what is called "The King's Room," a vaulted apartment, garnished with stags' antlers and similar trophies of the chase, and said by tradition to be the spot of Malcolm's murder, and I had an idea of the vicinity of the castle chapel.

In spite of the truth of history, the whole night-scene in Macbeth's castle rushed at once upon my mind, and struck my imagination ... I experienced sensations which, though not remarkable either for timidity or superstition, did not fail to affect me to the point of being disagreeable, while they were mingled at the same time with a strange and indescribably kind of pleasure, the recollection of which affords me gratification at this moment.

A generation later, a Scottish novelist, Mrs Oliphant (Margaret Wilson Oliphant, 1824-97), felt impelled to tell the story of Glamis as she imagined it might have happened; setting it in her own time, giving new names to the old castle and its family. Her account, entitled The Secret Chamber, *appeared in* Blackwood's Magazine *in December 1886; a good tale for Christmas.*

CHAPTER I

CASTLE GOWRIE is one of the most famous and interesting in all Scotland. It is a beautiful old house, to start with, — perfect in old feudal grandeur, with its clustered turrets and walls that could withstand an army, — its labyrinths, its hidden stairs, its long mysterious passages — passages that seem in many cases to lead to nothing, but of which no one can be too sure what they lead to. The front, with its fine gateway and flanking towers, is approached now by velvet lawns, and a peaceful, beautiful old avenue, with double rows of trees, like a cathedral; and the woods out of which these grey towers rise, look as soft and rich in foliage, if not so lofty in growth, as the groves of the South ... The Earls of Gowrie had been in the heat of every commotion that took place on or about the Highland line for more generations than any but a Celtic pen could record. Rebellions, revenges, insurrections, conspiracies, nothing in which blood was shed and lands lost, took place in Scotland, in which they had not had a share; and the annals of the house are very full, and not without many a stain. They had been a bold and vigorous race — with much evil in them, and some good; never insignificant, whatever else they might be. It could not be said, however, that they are remarkable nowadays. Since the first Stuart rising, known in Scotland as "the Fifteen," they have not done much that has been worth recording; but yet their family history has always been of an unusual kind. The Randolphs could not be called eccentric in themselves: on the contrary, when you knew them, they were at bottom a respectable race, full of all the country-gentleman virtues; and yet their public career, such as it was, had been marked by the strangest leaps and jerks of vicissitude. You would have said an impulsive, fanciful family — now making a grasp at some visionary advantage, now rushing into some wild speculation, now making a sudden sally into public life — but soon falling back into mediocrity, not able apparently, even when the impulse was purely selfish and mercenary, to keep it up. But this would not have been at all a true conception of the family character; their actual virtues were not of the imaginative order, and their freaks were a mystery to their friends. Nevertheless these freaks were what the general world was most aware of in the Randolph race. The late Earl had been a representative peer of Scotland (they had no English title), and had made quite a wonderful start, and for a year or two had seemed about to attain a very eminent place in Scotch affairs; but his ambition was found to have made use of some very equivocal modes of gaining influence, and he dropped accordingly at once and for ever from the political firmament. This was quite a common circumstance in the family. An apparently brilliant beginning, a discovery of evil means adopted for ambitious ends, a sudden subsidence, and the curious conclusion at the end of everything that this schemer, this unscrupulous speculator or politician, was a dull, good man after all - unambitious, contented, full of domestic kindness and benevolence. This family peculiarity made the history of the Randolphs a very strange one, broken by the oddest interruptions, and with no consistency in it. There was another circumstance, however, which attracted still more the wonder and observation of the public. For one who can appreciate such a recondite matter as family character, there are hundreds who are interested in a family secret, and this the house of Randolph possessed in perfection. It was a mystery which piqued the imagination and excited the interest of the entire country. The story went, that somewhere hid amid the massive walls and tortuous passages there was a secret chamber in Gowrie Castle. Everybody knew of its existence; but save the earl, his heir, and one other person, not of the family, but filling a confidential post in their service, no mortal knew where this mysterious hiding-place was. There had been countless guesses made at it, and expedients of all kinds invented to find it out. Every visitor who ever entered the old gateway, nay, even passing travellers who saw the turrets from the road, searched keenly for some trace of this mysterious chamber. But all guesses and researches were equally in vain . . .

It is wonderful how easily a family learns to pique itself upon any distinctive possession. A ghost is a sign of importance not to be despised; a haunted room is worth as much as a small farm to the complacency of the family that owns it. And no doubt the younger branches of the Gowrie family — the light-minded portion of the race — felt this, and were proud of their unfathomable secret, and felt a thrill of agreeable awe and piquant suggestion go through them, when they remembered the mysterious something which they did not know in their familiar home. That thrill ran through the entire circle of visitors, and children, and servants, when the Earl peremptorily forbade a projected improvement, or stopped a reckless exploration. They

51

looked at each other with a pleasurable shiver. "Did you hear!" they said. "He will not let Lady Gowrie have that closet she wants so much in that bit of wall. He sent the workmen about their business before they could touch it, though the wall is twenty feet thick if it is an inch; ah!" said the visitors, looking at each other; and this lively suggestion sent tinglings of excitement to their very finger-points; but even to his wife, mourning the commodious closet she had intended, the Earl made no explanations. For anything she knew, it might be there, next to her room, this mysterious lurking-place; and it may be supposed that this suggestion conveyed to Lady Gowrie's veins a thrill more keen and strange, perhaps too vivid to be pleasant. But she was not in the favoured or unfortunate number of those to whom the truth could be revealed.

I need not say what the different theories on the subject were. Some thought there had been a treacherous massacre there, and that the secret chamber was blocked by the skeletons of murdered guests, — a treachery no doubt covering the family with shame in its day, but so condoned by long softening of years as to have all the shame taken out of it. The Randolphs could not have felt their character affected by any such interesting historical record. They were not so morbidly sensitive. Some said, on the other hand, that Earl Robert, the wicked Earl, was shut up there in everlasting penance, playing cards with the devil for his soul. But it would have been too great a feather in the family cap to have thus got the devil, or even one of his angels, bottled up, as it were, and safely in hand, to make it possible that any lasting stigma could be connected with such a fact as this. What a thing it would be to know where to lay one's hand upon the Prince of Darkness, and prove him once for all, cloven foot and everything else, to the confusion of gainsayers!

So this was not to be received as a satisfactory solution, nor could any other be suggested which was more to the purpose . . .

This was how the matter stood when young John Randolph, Lord Lindores, came of age. He was a young man of great character and energy, not like the usual

Randolph strain — for, as we have said, the type of character common in this romantically-situated family, notwithstanding the erratic incidents common to them, was that of dullness and honesty, especially in their early days. But young Lindores was not so. He was honest and honourable, but not dull. He had gone through almost a remarkable course at school and at the university — not perhaps in quite the ordinary way of scholarship, but enough to attract men's eyes to him. He had made more than one great speech at the Union. He was full of ambition, and force, and life, intending all sorts of great things, and meaning to make his position a stepping-stone to all that was excellent in public life. Not for him the country-gentleman existence which was congenial to his father. The idea of succeeding to the family honours and becoming a Scotch peer, either represented or representative, filled him with horror; and filial piety in his case was made warm by all the energy of personal hopes when he prayed that his father might live, if not for ever, yet longer than any Lord Gowrie had lived for the last century or two. He was as sure of his election for the county the next time there was a chance, as anybody can be certain of anything; and in the meantime he meant to travel, to go to America, to go no one could tell where, seeking for instruction and experience, as is the manner of high-spirited young men with parliamentary tendancies in the present day ... He had made all his arrangements for his tour, which his father did not oppose. On the contrary, Lord Gowrie encouraged all those plans, though with an air of melancholy indulgence which his son could not understand. "It will do you good," he said, with a sigh. "Yes, yes, my boy; the best thing for you." All this settled accordingly for this journey, before he came home to go through the ceremonial performances of the coming of age, the dinner of the tenantry, the speeches, the congratulations, his father's banquet, his mother's ball. It was in summer, and the country was as gay as all the entertainments that were to be given in his honour. His friend who was going to accompany him on his tour, as he had accompanied him through a considerable portion of his life — Almeric Ffarrington, a young man of the same

53

aspirations — came up to Scotland with him for these festivities. And as they rushed through the night on the Great Northern Railway, in the intervals of two naps, they had a scrap of conversation as to these birthday glories. "It will be a bore, but it will not last long," said Lindores. They were both of the opinion that anything that did not produce information or promote culture was a bore.

"But is there not a revelation to be made to you, among all the other things you have to go through?" said Ffarrington. "Have not you to be introduced to the secret chamber, and all that sort of thing? I should like to be of the party there, Lindores."

"Ah," said the heir, "I had forgotten that part of it," which, however, was not the case. "Indeed I don't know if I am to be told. Even family dogmas are shaken nowadays."

"Oh, I should insist on that," said Ffarrington, lightly. "It is not many who have the chance of paying such a visit — better than Home and all the mediums. I should insist upon that."

"I have no reason to suppose that it has any connection with Home or the mediums," said Lindores, slightly nettled. He was himself an *esprit fort*; but a mystery in one's own family is not like vulgar mysteries. He liked it to be respected.

"Oh, no offence," said his companion. "I have always thought that a railway train would be a great chance for the spirits. If one was to show suddenly in that vacant seat beside you, what a triumphant proof of their existence that would be! but they don't take advantage of their opportunities."

Lindores could not tell what it was that made him think at that moment of a portrait he had seen in a back room at the castle of old Earl Robert, the wicked Earl. It was a bad portrait — a daub — a copy made by an amateur of the genuine portrait, which, out of horror of Earl Robert and his wicked ways, had been removed by some intermediate lord from its place in the gallery. Lindores had never seen the original — nothing but this daub of a copy. Yet somehow this face occurred to him by some strange link of association — seemed to come into his eyes as his friend spoke. A slight shiver ran over him. It was strange. He made

54

no reply to Ffarrington, but set himself to think how it could be that the latent presence in his mind of some anticipation of this approaching disclosure, touched into life by his friend's suggestion, should have called out of his memory a momentary realisation of the acknowledged magician of the family. This sentence is full of long words; but unfortunately long words are required in such a case. And the process was very simple when you traced it out. It was the clearest case of unconscious cerebration. He shut his eyes by way of securing privacy while he thought it out; and being tired, and not at all alarmed by his unconscious cerebration, before he opened them again fell fast asleep.

And his birthday, which was the day following his arrival at Glenlyon, was a very busy day. He had not time to think of anything but the immediate occupations of the moment. Public and private greetings, congratulations, offerings, poured upon him. The Gowries were popular in this generation, which was far from being usual in the family. Lady Gowrie was kind and generous, with that kindness which comes from the heart, and which is the only kindness likely to impress the keen-sighted popular judgment; and Lord Gowrie had but little of the equivocal reputation of his predecessors. They could be splendid now and then on great occasions, though in general they were homely enough; all which the public likes. It was a bore, Lindores said; but yet the young man did not dislike the honours, and the adulation, and all the hearty speeches and good wishes. It is sweet to a young man to feel himself the centre of all hopes ... He was almost solemnised by his own position — so young, looked up to by so many people — so many hopes depending on him; and yet it was quite natural. His father, however, was still more solemnised than Lindores — and this was strange, to say the least. His face grew graver and graver as the day went on, till it almost seemed as if he were dissatisfied with his son's popularity, or had some painful thought weighing on his mind. He was restless and eager for the termination of the dinner, and to get rid of his guests; and as soon as they were gone, showed an equal anxiety that his son should retire too. "Go to bed at once, as a favour to me," Lord Gowrie said. "You will have a great deal of fatigue — to-morrow." "You need not be afraid for me, sir," said Lindores, half affronted; but he obeyed, being tired. He had not once thought of the secret to be disclosed to him, through all that long day. But when he woke suddenly with a start in the middle of the night, to find the candles all lighted in his room, and his father standing by his bedside, Lindores instantly thought of it, and in a moment felt that the leading event — the chief incident of all that had happened — was going to take place now.

CHAPTER II

LORD GOWRIE was very grave, and very pale. He was standing with his hand on his son's shoulder to wake him; his dress was unchanged from the moment they had parted. And the sight of this formal costume was very bewildering to the young man as he started up in his bed. But next moment he seemed to know exactly how it was, and, more than that, to have known it all his life. Explanation seemed unnecessary. At any other moment, in any other place, a man would be startled to be suddenly woke up in the middle of the night. But Lindores had no such feeling; he did not even ask a question, but sprang up, and fixed his eyes, taking in all the strange circumstances, on his father's face.

"Get up, my boy," said Lord Gowrie, "and dress as quickly as you can; it is full time. I have lighted your candles, and your things are all ready. You have had a good long sleep."

Even now he did not ask, What is it? as under any other circumstances. He got up without a word, with an impulse of nervous speed and rapidity of movement such as only excitement can give, and dressed himself, his father helping him silently. It was curious scene: the room gleaming with lights, the silence, the hurried toilet, the stillness of deep night all around. The house, though so full, and with the echoes of festivity but just over, was quiet as if there was not a creature within it — more quiet, indeed, for the stillness of vacancy is not half so impressive as the stillness of hushed and slumbering life.

Lord Gowrie went to the table when this first step was over, and poured out a glass of wine from a bottle which stood there, — a rich golden-coloured, perfumy wine, which sent its scent through the room. "You will want all your strength," he said; "take this before you go. It is the famous Imperial Tokay; there is only a little left, and you will want all your strength."

Lindores took the wine; he had never drunk any like it before, and the peculiar fragrance remained in his mind, as perfumes so often do, with a whole world of association in them. His father's eyes dwelt upon him with a melancholy sympathy. "You are going to encounter the greatest trial of your life," he said; and taking the young man's hand into his, felt his pulse. "It is quick, but it is quite firm and you have had a good long sleep." Then he did what it needs a great deal of pressure to induce an Englishman to do, — he kissed his son on the cheek. "God bless you!" he said, faltering. "Come, now, everything is ready, Lindores."

He took up in his hand a small lamp, which he had apparently brought with him, and led the way. By this time Lindores began to feel himself again, and to wake to the consciousness of all his own superiorities and enlightenments. The simple sense that he was one of the members of a family with a mystery, and that the moment of his personal encounter with this special power of darkness had come, had been the first thrilling, overwhelming thought. But now as he followed his father, Lindores began to remember that he himself was not altogether like other men; that there was that in him which would make it natural that he should throw some light, hitherto unthought of, upon this carefully-preserved darkness. What secret even there might be in it — secret of hereditary tendency, of psychic force, of mental conformation, or of some curious combination of circumstances at once more and less potent that these — it was for him to find out. He gathered all his forces about him, reminded himself of modern enlightenment, and bade his nerves be steel to all vulgar horrors. He, too, felt his own pulse as he followed his father. To spend the night perhaps amongst the skeletons of that old-world massacre, and to repent the sins of his ancestors — to be brought within the range of some optical illusion believed in hitherto by all the generations, and which, no

57

doubt, was of a startling kind, or his father would not look so serious, — any of these he felt himself quite strong to encounter. His heart and spirit rose. A young man has but seldom the opportunity of distinguishing himself so early in his career; and his was such a chance as occurs to very few. No doubt it was something that would be extremely trying to the nerves and imagination. He called up all his powers to vanquish both. And along with this call upon himself to exertion, there was the less serious impulse of curiosity: he would see at last what the Secret Chamber was, where it was, how it fitted into the labyrinths of the old house. This he tried to put in its due place as a most intersting object. He said to himself that he would willingly have gone a long journey at any time to be present at such an exploration; and there is no doubt that in other circumstances a secret chamber, with probably some unthought-of historical interest in it, would have been a very fascinating discovery. He tried very hard to excite himself about this; but it was curious how fictitious he felt the interest, and how conscious he was that it was an effort to feel any curiosity at all on the subject. The fact was, that the Secret Chamber was entirely secondary — thrown back, as all accessories are, by a more pressing interest. The overpowering thought of what was in it drove aside all healthy, natural curiosity about itself.

It must not be supposed, however, that the father and son had a long way to go to have time for all these thoughts. Thoughts travel at lightning speed, and there was abundant leisure for this between the time they had left the door of Lindores' room and gone down the corridor, no further off than to Lord Gowrie's own chamber, naturally one of the chief rooms of the house. Nearly opposite this, a few steps further on, was a little neglected room devoted to lumber, with which Lindores had been familiar all his life. Why this nest of old rubbish, dust, and cobwebs should be so near the bedroom of the head of the house had been a matter of surprise to many people — to the guests who saw it while exploring, and to each new servant in succession who planned an attack upon its ancient stores, scandalised by finding it to have been neglected by their predecessors. All their attempts to clear it out had, however, been resisted, nobody could tell how, or indeed thought it worth while to inquire. As for Lindores, he had been used to the place from his childhood, and therefore accepted it as the most natural thing in the world. He had been in and out a hundred times in his play. And it was here, he remembered suddenly, that he had seen the bad picture of Earl Robert which had so curiously come into his eyes on his journeying here, by a mental movement which he had identified at once as unconscious cerebration. The first feeling in his mind, as his father went to the open door of this lumber-room, was a mixture of amusement and surprise. What was he going to pick up there? some old pentacle, some amulet or scrap of antiquated magic to act as armour against the evil one? But Lord Gowrie, going on and setting down the lamp on the table, turned round upon his son with a face of agitation and pain which barred all further amusement: he grasped him by the hand, crushing it between his own. "Now my boy, my dear son," he said, in tones that were scarcely audible. His countenance was full of the dreary pain of a looker-on — one who has no share in the excitement of personal danger, but has the more terrible part of watching those who are in deadliest peril. He was a powerful man, and his large form shook with emotion; great beads of moisture stood upon his forehead. An old sword with a cross handle lay upon a dusty chair among other dusty and battered relics. "Take this with you," he said, in the same inaudible, breathless way — whether as a weapon, whether as a religious symbol, Lindores could not guess. The young man took it mechanically. His father pushed open a door which it seemed to him he had never seen before, and led him into another vaulted chamber. Here even the limited powers of speech Lord Gowrie had retained seemed to forsake him, and his voice became a mere hoarse murmur in his throat. For want of speech he pointed to another door in the further corner of this small vacant room, gave him to understand by a gesture that he was to knock there, and then went back into the lumber-room. The door into this was left open, and a faint glimmer of the lamp shed light into this little intermediate place — this debatable land between the seen and the unseen. In spite of himself, Lindores' heart began to beat. He made a breathless pause, feeling his head go round. He held the old sword in his hand, not knowing what it was. Then, summoning all his courage, he went forward and knocked at the closed door. His knock was not loud, but it seemed to echo all over the silent house. Would everybody hear and wake, and rush to see what had happened? This caprice of imagination seized upon him, ousting all the firmer thoughts, the steadfast calm of mind with which he ought to have encountered the mystery. Would they all rush in, in wild *déshabille*, in terror and dismay, before the door opened? How long it was of opening! He touched the panel with his hand again. — This time there was no delay. In a moment, as if thrown suddenly open by some one within, the door moved. It opened just wide enough to let him enter, stopping half-way as if some one invisible held it, wide enough for welcome, but no more. Lindores stepped across the threshold with a beating heart. What was he about to see? the skeletons of the murdered victims? a ghostly charnel-house full of bloody traces of crime? He seemed to be hurried and pushed in as he made that step. What was this world of mystery into which he was plunged — what was it he saw?

He saw — nothing — except what was agreeable enough to behold, — an antiquated room hung with tapestry, very old tapestry of rude design, its colours faded into softness and harmony; between its folds here and there a panel of carved wood, rude too in design, with traces of half-worn gilding; a table covered with strange instruments, parchments, chemical tubes, and curious machinery, all with a quaintness of form and dimness of material that spoke of age. A heavy old velvet cover, thick with embroidery faded almost out of all colour, was on the table; on the wall above it, something that looked like a very old Venetian mirror, the glass so dim and crusted that it scarcely reflected at all; on the floor an old soft Persian carpet, worn into a vague blending of all colours. This was all that he thought he saw. His heart, which had been thumping so loud as almost to choke him, stopped that tremendous upward and downward motion like a steam piston; and he grew calm. Perfectly still, dim, unoccupied: yet not so dim either;

Lindores stepped across the threshold

there was no apparent source of light, no windows, curtains of tapestry drawn everywhere — no lamp visible, no fire — and yet a kind of strange light which made everything quite clear. He looked round, trying to smile at his terrors, trying to say to himself that it was the most curious place he had ever seen — that he must show Ffarrington some of that tapestry — that he must really bring away a panel of that carving, — when he suddenly saw that the door was shut by which he had entered — nay, more than shut, undiscernible, covered like all the rest of the walls by that strange tapestry. At this his heart began to beat again in spite of him. He looked round once more, and woke up to more vivid being with a sudden start. Had his eyes been incapable of vision on his first entrance? Unoccupied? Who was that in the great chair?

It seemed to Lindores that he had seen neither the chair nor the man when he came in. There they were, however, solid and unmistakable; the chair carved like the panels, the man seated in front of the table. He looked at Lindores with a calm and open gaze, inspecting him. The young man's heart seemed in his throat fluttering like a bird, but he was brave, and his mind made one final effort to break this spell. He tried to speak, labouring with a voice that would not sound, and with lips too parched to form a word. "I see how it is," was what he wanted to say. It was Earl Robert's face that was looking at him; and startled as he was, he dragged forth his philosophy to support him. What could it be but optical delusions, unconscious cerebration, occult seizure by the impressed and struggling mind of this one countenance? But he could not hear himself speak any word as he stood convulsed, struggling with dry lips and choking voice.

The Appearance smiled, as if knowing his thoughts — not unkindly, not malignly — with a certain amusement mingled with scorn. Then he spoke, and the sound seemed to breathe through the room not like any voice that Lindores had ever heard, a kind of utterance of the place, like the rustle of the air or the ripple of the sea. "You will learn better to-night: this is no phantom of your brain; it is I."

"In God's name," cried the young man in his soul; he did

not know whether the words ever got into the air or not, if there was any air; — "in God's name, who are you?"

The figure rose as if coming to him to reply; and Lindores, overcome by the apparent approach, struggled into utterance. A cry came from him — he heard it this time — and even in his extremity felt a pang the more to hear the terror in his own voice. But he did not flinch, he stood desperate, all his strength concentrated in the act; he neither turned nor recoiled. Vaguely gleaming through his mind came the thought that to be thus brought in contact with the unseen was the experiment to be most desired on earth, the final settlement of a hundred questions; but his faculties were not sufficiently under command to entertain it. He only stood firm, that was all.

And the figure did not approach him; after a moment it subsided back again into the chair — subsided, for no sound, not the faintest, accompanied its movements. It was the form of a man of middle age, the hair white, but the beard only crisped with grey, the features those of the picture — a familiar face, more or less like all the Randolphs; but with an air of domination and power altogether unlike that of the race. He was dressed in a long robe of dark colour, embroidered with strange lines and angles. There was nothing repellent or terrible in his air — nothing except the noiselessness, the calm, the absolute stillness, which was as much in the place as in him, to keep up the involuntary trembling of the beholder. His expression was full of dignity and thoughtfulness, and not malignant or unkind. He might have been the kindly patriarch of the house, watching over its fortunes in a seclusion he had chosen. The pulses that had been beating in Lindores were stilled. What was his panic for? a gleam even of self-ridicule took possession of him, to be standing there like an absurd hero of antiquated romance with the rusty, dusty sword — good for nothing, surely not for use against this noble old magician — in his hand —

"You are right," said the voice, once more answering his thoughts; "what could you do with that sword against me, young Lindores? Put it by. Why should my children meet me like an enemy? You are my flesh and blood. Give me your hand."

A shiver ran through the young man's frame. The hand that was held out to him was large and shapely and white, with a straight line across the palm — a family token upon which the Randolphs prided themselves — a friendly hand; and the face smiled upon him, fixing him with those calm, profound, blue eyes. "Come," said the voice. The word seemed to fill the place, melting upon him from every corner, whispering round him with softest persuasion. He was lulled and calmed in spite of himself. Spirit or no spirit, why should not he accept this proffered courtesy? What harm could come of it? The chief thing that retained him was the dragging of the old sword, heavy and useless, which he held mechanically, but which some internal feeling — he could not tell what — prevented him from putting down. Superstition, was it?

"Yes, that is superstition," said his ancestor, serenely; "put it down and come."

"You know my thoughts," said Lindores; "I did not speak."

"Your mind spoke, and spoke justly. Put down that emblem of brute force and superstition together. Here it is the intelligence that is supreme. Come."

Lindores stood doubtful. He was calm; the power of thought was restored to him. If this benevolent venerable patriarch was all he seemed, why his father's terror? why the secrecy in which his being was involved? His own mind, though calm, did not seem to act in the usual way. Thoughts seemed to be driven across it as by a wind. One of these came to him suddenly now —

"How there looked him in the face,
    An angel beautiful and bright,
And how he knew it was a fiend."

The words were not ended, when Earl Robert replied suddenly with impatience in his voice, "Fiends are of the fancy of men; like angels and other follies. I am your father. You know me; and you are mine, Lindores. I have power beyond what you can understand; but I want flesh and blood to reign and to enjoy. Come, Lindores!"

He put out his other hand. The action, the look, were

64

those of kindness, almost of longing, and the face was
familiar, the voice was that of the race. Supernatural! was it
supernatural that this man should live here shut up for ages?
and why? and how? Was there any explanation of it? The
young man's brain began to reel. He could not tell which was
real — the life he had left half an hour ago, or this. He tried
to look round him, but could not; his eyes were caught by
those other kindred eyes, which seemed to dilate and deepen
as he looked at them, and drew him with a strange
compulsion. He felt himself yielding, swaying towards the
strange being who thus invited him. What might happen if
he yielded? And he could not turn away, he could not tear
himself from the fascination of those eyes. With a sudden
strange impulse which was half despair and half a
bewildering half-conscious desire to try one potency against
another, he thrust forward the cross of the old sword
between him and those appealing hands. "In the name of
God!" he said.

Lindores never could tell whether it was that he himself
grew faint, and that the dimness of swooning came into his
eyes after this violence and strain of emotion, or if it was his
spell that worked. But there was an instantaneous change.
Everything swam around him for the moment, a giddiness
and blindness seized him, and he saw nothing but the vague
outlines of the room, empty as when he entered it. But
gradually his consciousness came back, and he found
himself standing on the same spot as before, clutching the
old sword, and gradually, as though a dream, recognised the
same figure emerging out of the mist which — was it solely in
his own eyes? — had enveloped everything. But it was no
longer in the same attitude. The hands which had been
stretched out of him were busy now with some of the strange
instruments on the table, moving about, now in the action of
writing, now as if managing the keys of a telegraph.
Lindores felt that his brain was all atwist and set wrong; but
he was still a human being of his century. He thought of the
telegraph with a keen thrill of curiosity in the midst of his
reviving sensations. What communication was this which
was going on before his eyes? The magician worked on. He
had his face turned towards his victim, but his hands moved

with unceasing activity. And Lindores, as he grew
accustomed to the position, began to weary — to feel like a
neglected suitor waiting for an audience. To be wound up to
such a strain of feeling, then left to wait, was intolerable;
impatience seized upon him. What circumstances can exist,
however horrible, in which a human being will not feel
impatience? He made a great many efforts to speak before
he could succeed. It seemed to him that his body felt more
fear than he did — that his muscles were contracted, his
throat parched, his tongue refusing its office, although his
mind was unaffected and undismayed. At last he found an
utterance in spite of all resistance of his flesh and blood.

"Who are you?" he said hoarsely. "You that live here and
oppress this house?"

The vision raised its eyes full upon him, with again that
strange shadow of a smile, mocking yet not unkind. "Do you
remember me," he said, "on your journey here?"

"That was — a delusion." The young man gasped for
breath.

"More like that you are a delusion. You have lasted but
one-and-twenty years, and I — for centuries."

"How? For centuries   and why? Answer me   are you
man or demon?" creid Lindores, tearing the words, as he
felt, out of his own throat. "Are you living or dead?"

The magician looked at him with the same intense gaze as
before. "Be on my side, and you shall know everything,
Lindores. I want one of my own race. Others I could have in
plenty; but I want *you*. A Randolph, a Randolph! and *you*.
Dead! do I seem dead? You shall have everything — more
than dreams can give — if you will be on my side."

Can he give what he has not? was the thought that ran
through the mind of Lindores. But he could not speak it.
Something that choked and stifled him was in his throat.

"Can I give what I have not? I have everything — power,
the one thing worth having; and you shall have more than
power, for you are young — my son! Lindores!"

To argue was natural, and gave the young man strength.
"Is this life," he said, "here? What is all your power worth —
here? To sit for ages, and make a race unhappy?"

A momentary convulsion came across the still face. "You

66

scorn me," he cried, with an appearance of emotion, "because you do not understand how I move the world. Power! 'Tis more than fancy can grasp. And you shall have it!" said the wizard, with what looked like a show of enthusiasm. He seemed to come nearer, to grow larger. He put forth his hand again, this time so close that it seemed impossible to escape. And a crowd of wishes seemed to rush upon the mind of Lindores. What harm to try if this might be true? To try what it meant — perhaps nothing, delusions, vain show, and then there could be no harm; or perhaps there was knowledge to be had, which was power. Try, try, try! the air buzzed about him. The room seemed full of voices urging him. His bodily frame rose into a tremendous whirl of excitement, his veins seemed to swell to bursting, his lips seemed to force a yes, in spite of him, quivering as they came apart. The hiss of the *s* seemed in his ears. He changed it into the name which was a spell too, and cried "Help me, God!" not knowing why.

Then there came another pause — he felt as if he had been dropped from something that had held him, and had fallen, and was faint. The excitement had been more than he could bear. Once more everything swam around him, and he did not know where he was. Had he escaped altogether? was the first waking wonder of consciousness in his mind. But when he could think and see again, he was still in the same spot, surrounded by the old curtains and the carved panels — but alone. He felt, too, that he was able to move, but the strangest dual consciousness was in him throughout all the rest of his trial. His body felt to him as a frightened horse feels to be a traveller at night — a thing separate from him, more frightened than he was — starting aside at every step, seeing more than its master. His limbs shook with fear and weakness, almost refusing to obey the action of his will, trembling under him with jerks aside when he compelled himself to move. The hair stood upright on his head — every finger trembled as with palsy — his lips, his eyelids, quivered with nervous agitation. But his mind was strong, stimulated to a desperate calm. He dragged himself round the room, he crossed the very spot where the magician had been — all was vacant, silent, clear. Had he vanquished the enemy? This thought came into his mind with an involuntary triumph. The old strain of feeling came back. Such efforts might be produced, perhaps, only by imagination, by excitement, by delusion —

Lindores looked up, by a sudden attraction he could not tell what; and the blood suddenly froze in his veins that had been so boiling and fermenting. Some one was looking at him from the old mirror on the wall. A face not human and life-like, like that of the inhabitant of this place, but ghostly and terrible, like one of the dead; and while he looked, a crowd of other faces came behind, all looking at him, some mournfully, some with a menace in their terrible eyes. The mirror did not change, but within its small dim space seemed to contain an innumerable company, crowded above and below, all with one gaze at him. His lips dropped apart with a gasp of horror. More and more and more! He was standing close by the table when this crowd came. Then all at once there was laid upon him a cold hand. He turned; close to his side, brushing him with his robe, holding him fast by the arm, sat Earl Robert in his great chair. A shriek came from the young man's lips. He seemed to hear it echoing away into unfathomable distance. The cold touch penetrated to his very soul.

"Do you try spells upon me, Lindores? That is a tool of the past. You shall have something better to work with. And are you so sure of whom you call upon? If there is such a one, why should He help you who never called on Him before?"

Lindores could not tell if these words were spoken; it was a communication rapid as the thoughts in the mind. And he felt as if something answered that was not all himself. He seemed to stand passive and hear the argument. "Does God reckon with a man in trouble, whether he has ever called to Him before? I call now" (now he felt it was himself that said): "go, evil spirit! — go, dead and cursed! — go, in the name of God!"

He felt himself flung violently against the wall. A faint laugh, stifled in the throat, and followed by a groan, rolled round the room; the old curtains seemed to open here and there, and flutter, as if with comings and goings. Lindores leaned with his back against the wall, and all his senses

68

restored to him. He felt blood trickle down his neck; and in this contact once more with the physical, his body, in its madness of fright, grew manageable. For the first time he felt wholly master of himself. Though the magician was standing in his place, a great, majestic, appalling figure, he did not shrink. "Liar!" he cried, in a voice that rang and echoed as in natural air — "clinging to miserable life like a worm — like a reptile; promising all things, having nothing, but this den, unvisited by the light of day. Is this your power — your superiority to men who die? is it for this that you oppress a race, and make a house unhappy? I vow, in God's name, your reign is over! You and your secret shall last no more."

There was no reply. But Lindores felt his terrible ancestor's eyes getting once more that mesmeric mastery over him which had already almost overcome his powers. He must withdraw his own, or perish. He had a human horror of turning his back upon that watchful adversary: to face him seemed the only safety; but to face him was to be conquered. Slowly, with a pang indescribable, he tore himself from that gaze: it seemed to drag his eyes out of their sockets, his heart out of his bosom. Resolutely, with the daring of desperation, he turned round to the spot where he entered — the spot where no door was, — hearing already in anticipation the step after him — feeling the grip that would crush and smother his exhausted life — but too desperate to care.

CHAPTER III

Lord Gowrie sat among the dust and cobwebs, his lamp flaring idly into the blue morning. He had heard his son's human voice, though nothing more; and he expected to have him brought out by invisible hands, as had happened to himself, and left lying in long deathly swoon outside that mystic door. This was how it had happened to heir after hair, as told from father to son, one after another, as the secret came down. One or two bearers of the name of Lindores had never recovered; most of them had been saddened and subdued for life. He remembered sadly the freshness of existence which had never come back to himself; the hopes that had never blossomed again; the assurance with which never more he had been able to go about the world. And now his son would be as himself — the glory gone out of his living — his ambitions, his aspirations wrecked. He had not been endowed as his boy was — he had been a plain, honest man, and nothing more; but experience and life had given him wisdom enough to smile by times at the coquetries of mind in which Lindores indulged. Were they all over now, those freaks of young intelligence, those enthusiams of the soul? The curse of the house had come upon him — the magnetism of that strange presence, ever living, ever watchful, present in all the family history. His heart was sore for his son; and yet along with this there was a certain consolation to him in having hence-forward a partner in the secret — some one to whom he could talk of it as he had not been able to talk since his own father died. Almost all the mental struggles which Gowrie had known had been connected with this mystery; and he had been obliged to hide them in his bosom — to conceal them even when they rent him in two. Now he had a partner in his trouble. This was what he was thinking as he sat through the night. How slowly the moments passed! He was not aware of the daylight coming in. After a while even thought got suspended in listening. Was not the time nearly over? He rose and began to pace about the encumbered space, which was but a step or two in extent. There was an old cupboard in the wall, in which there were restoratives — pungent essences and cordials, and fresh water which he had himself brought — everything was ready; presently the ghastly body of his boy, half dead, would be thrust forth into his care.

But this was not how it happened. While he waited, so intent that his whole frame seemed to be capable of hearing, he heard the closing of the door, boldly shut with a sound that rose in muffled echoes through the house, and Lindores himself appeared, ghastly indeed as a dead man, but walking upright and firmly, the lines of his face drawn, and his eyes staring. Lord Gowrie uttered a cry. He was more alarmed by this unexpected return than by the helpless prostration of the swoon which he had expected. He recoiled from his son as if he too had been a spirit. "Lindores!" he cried; was it

Lindores, or some one else in his place? The boy seemed as if he did not see him. He went straight forward to where the water stood on the dusty table, and took a great draught, then turned to the door. "Lindores!" said his father, in miserable anxiety; "don't you know me?" Even then the young man only half looked at him, and put out a hand almost as cold as the hand that had clutched himself in the Secret Chamber; a faint smile came upon his face. "Don't stay here," he whispered; "come! come!"

Lord Gowrie drew his son's arm within his own, and felt the thrill through and through him of nerves strained beyond mortal strength. He could scarcely keep up with him as he stalked along the corridor to his room, stumbling as if he could not see, yet swift as an arrow. When they reached his room he turned and closed and locked the door, then laughed as he staggered to the bed. "That will not keep him out, will it?" he said.

"Lindores," said his father. "I expected to find you unconscious I am almost more frightened to find you like this. I need not ask if you have seen him —"

"Oh, I have seen him. The old liar! Father, promise to expose him, to turn him out — promise to clear out that accursed old nest! It is our own fault. Why have we left such a place shut out from the eye of day? Isn't there something in the Bible about those who do evil hating the light?"

"Lindores! you don't often quote the Bible."

"No, I suppose not; but there is more truth in — many things than we thought."

"Lie down," said the anxious father. "Take some of this wine — try to sleep."

"Take it away; give me no more of that devil's drink. Talk to me — that's better. Did you go through it all the same, poor papa? — and hold me fast. You are warm — you are honest!" he cried. He put forth his hands over his father's, warming them with the contact. He put his cheek like a child against his father's arm. He gave a faint laugh, with the tears in his eyes. "Warm and honest," he repeated. "Kind flesh and blood! and did you go through it all the same?"

"My boy!" cried the father, feeling his heart glow and swell over the son who had been parted from him for years by that development of young manhood and ripening intellect which so often severs and loosens the ties of home. Lord Gowrie had felt that Lindores half despised his simple mind and duller imagination; but this childlike clinging overcame him, and tears stood in his eyes. "I fainted, I suppose. I never knew how it ended. They made what they like of me. But you, my brave boy, you came out of your own will."

Lindores shivered. "I fled!" he said. "No honour in that. I had not courage to face him longer. I will tell you by-and-by. But I want to know about you."

What an ease it was to the father to speak! For years and years this had been shut up in his breast. It had made him lonely in the midst of his friends.

"Thank God," he said, "that I can speak to you, Lindores. Often and often I have been tempted to tell your mother. But why should I make her miserable? She knows there is something; she knows when I see him, but she knows no more."

"When you see him?" Lindores raised himself, with a return of his first ghastly look, in his bed. Then he raised his clenched fist wildly, and shook it in the air. "Vile devil coward, deceiver!"

"Oh hush, hush, hush, Lindores! God help us! what troubles you may bring!"

"And God help me, whatever troubles I bring," said the young man. "I defy him, father. An accursed being like that must be less, not more powerful, than we are — with God to back us. Only stand by me; stand by me —"

"Hush, Lindores! You don't feel it yet — never to get out of hearing of him all your life! He will make you pay for it — if not now, after; when you remember he is there, whatever happens, knowing everything! But I hope it will not be so bad with you as with me, my poor boy. God help you indeed if it is, for you have more imagination and more mind. I am able to forget him sometimes when I am occupied — when in the hunting-field, going across country. But you are not a hunting man, my poor boy," said Lord Gowrie, with a curious mixture of a regret, which was less serious than the other. Then he lowered his voice. "Lindores, this is what has happened to me since the moment I gave him my hand."

"I did not give him my hand."

"You did not give him your hand? God bless you, my boy! You stood out?" he cried, with tears again rushing to his eyes; "and they say — they say — but I don't know if there is any truth in it." Lord Gowrie got up from his son's side, and walked up and down with excited steps. "If there should be truth in it! Many people think the whole thing is a fancy. If there should be truth in it, Lindores!"

"In what, father?"

"They say, if he is once resisted his power is broken — once refused. *You* could stand against him — you! Forgive me, my boy, as I hope God will forgive me, to have thought so little of His best gifts," cried Lord Gowrie, coming back with wet eyes; and stooping, he kissed his son's hand. "I thought you would be more shaken by being more mind than body," he said, humbly. "I thought if I could but have saved you from the trial; and *you* are the conqueror!"

"Am I the conqueror? I think all my bones are broken, father — out of their sockets," said the young man, in a low voice. "I think I shall go to sleep."

"Yes, rest, my boy. It is the best thing for you," said the father, though with a pang of momentary disappointment. Lindores fell back upon the pillow. He was so pale that there were moments when the anxious watcher thought him not sleeping but dead. He put his hand out feebly, and grasped his father's hand. "Warm — honest," he said, with a feeble smile about his lips, and fell asleep . . .

By-and-by, when Lindores' grasp relaxed, and he [Lord Gowrie] got his hand free, he got up from his son's bedside, and put out the lamp, putting it carefully out of the way. With equal care he put away the wine from the table, and gave the room its ordinary aspect, softly opening a window to let in the fresh air of the morning. The park lay fresh in the early sunshine, still, except for the twittering of the birds, refreshed with dews, and shining in that soft radiance of the morning which is over before mortal cares are stirring. Never, perhaps, had Gowrie looked out upon the beautiful world around his house without a thought of the weird existence which was going on so near to him, which had gone on for centuries, shut up out of sight of the sunshine. The Secret Chamber had been present with him since ever he saw it. He had never been able to get free of the spell of it. He had felt himself watched, surrounded, spied upon, day after day, since he was of the age of Lindores, and that was thirty years ago. He turned it all over in his mind, as he stood there and his son slept. It had been on his lips to tell it all to his boy, who had now come to inherit the enlightenment of his race. And it was a disappointment to him to have it all forced back again, and silence imposed upon him once more. Would he care to hear it when he woke? would he not rather, as Lord Gowrie remembered to have done himself, thrust the thought as far as he could away from him, and endeavour to forget for the moment — until the time came when he would not be permitted to forget? He had been like that himself, he recollected now. He had not wished to hear his own father's tale. "I remember," he said to himself; "I remember" — turning over everything in his mind — if Lindores might only be willing to hear the story when he woke! But then he himself had not been willing when he was Lindores, and he could understand his son, and could not blame him; but it would be a disappointment. He was thinking this when he heard Lindores' voice calling him. He went back hastily to his bedside. It was strange to see him in his evening dress with his worn face, in the fresh light of the morning, which poured in at every crevice. "Does my mother know?" said Lindores; "what will she think?"

"She knows something; she knows you have some trial to go through. Most likely she will be praying for us both; that's the way of women," said Lord Gowrie, with the tremulous tenderness which comes into a man's voice sometimes when he speaks of a good wife. "I'll go and ease her mind, and tell her all is well over ——"

"Not yet. Tell me first," said the young man, putting his hand upon his father's arm.

What an ease it was! "I was not so good to my father," he thought to himself, with sudden penitence for the long-past, long-forgotten fault, which, indeed, he had never realised as a fault before. And then he told his son what had been the story of his life — how he had scarcely ever sat alone without

74

feeling, from some corner of the room, from behind some curtain, those eyes upon him; and how, in the difficulties of his life, that secret inhabitant of the house had been present, sitting by him and advising him. "Whenever there has been anything to do; when there has been a question between two ways, all in a moment I have seen him by me: I feel when he is coming. It does not matter where I am — here or anywhere — as soon as ever there is a question of family business; and always he persuades me to the wrong way, Lindores. Sometimes I yield to him, how can I help it? He makes everything so clear; he makes wrong seem right . . . Lindores, Lindores! when there is any business it makes my heart sick. I know he will come, and advise wrong, and tell me — something I will repent after."

"The thing to do is to decide beforehand, that, good or bad, you will not take his advice."

Lord Gowrie shivered. "I am not strong like you, or clever; I cannot resist. Sometimes I repent in time and don't do it; and then! But for your mother and you children, there is many a day I would not have given a farthing for my life."

"Father," said Lindores, springing from his bed, "two of us together can do many things. Give me your word to clear out this cursed den of darkness this very day."

"Lindores, hush, hush, for the sake of heaven!"

"I will not, for the sake of heaven! Throw is open — let everybody who likes see it — make an end of the secret — pull down everything, curtains, walls. What do you say? — sprinkle holy water? Are you laughing at me?"

"I did not speak," said Earl Gowrie, growing very pale, and grasping his son's arm with both his hands. "Hush, boy; do you think he does not hear?"

And then there was a low laugh close to them — so close that both shrank; a laugh no louder than a breath.

"Did you laugh — father?"

"No, Lindores." Lord Gowrie had his eyes fixed. He was as pale as the dead. He held his son tight for a moment; then his gaze and his grasp relaxed, and he fell back feebly in a chair.

"You see!" he said; "whatever we do it will be the same; we are under his power.

And then there ensued the blank pause with which baffled men confront a hopeless situation. But at that moment the first faint stirrings of the house — a window being opened, a bar undone, a movement of feet, and subdued voices — became audible in the stillness of the morning. Lord Gowrie roused himself at once. "We must not be found like this," he said; "we must not show how we have spent the night. It is over, thank God! and oh, my boy, forgive me! I am thankful there are two of us to bear it; it makes the burden lighter — though I ask your pardon humbly for saying so. I would have saved you if I could, Lindores."

"I don't wish to have been saved; but *I* will not bear it. I will end it," the young man said, with an oath out of which his emotion took all profanity. His father said, "Hush, hush." With a look of terror and pain, he left him; and yet there was a thrill of tender pride in his mind. How brave the boy was! even after he had been *there*. Could it be that this would all come to nothing, as every other attempt to resist had done before?

"I suppose you know all about it now, Lindores," said his friend Ffarrington, after breakfast; "luckily for us who are going over the house. What a glorious old place it is!"

"I don't think that Lindores enjoys the glorious old place to-day," said another of the guests under his breath. "How pale he is! He doesn't look as if he had slept."

"I will take you over every nook where I have ever been," said Lindores. He looked at his father with almost command in his eyes. "Come with me, all of you. We shall have no more secrets here."

"Are you mad?" said his father in his ear.

"Never mind," cried the young man. "Oh, trust me; I will do it with judgment. Is everybody ready?" There was an excitement about him that half frightened, half roused the party. They all rose, eager, yet doubtful. His mother came to him and took his arm.

"Lindores! you will do nothing to vex your father; don't make him unhappy. I don't know your secrets, you two; but look, he has enough to bear."

"I want you to know our secrets, mother. Why should we

76

have secrets from you?"

Why, indeed?" she said, with tears in her eyes. "But, Lindores, my dearest boy, don't make it worse for *him*."

"I give you my word, I will be wary," he said; and she left him to go to his father, who followed the party, with an anxious look upon his face.

"Are you coming, too?" he asked.

"I? No; I will not go: but trust him — trust the boy, John."

"He can do nothing; he will not be able to do anything," he said.

And thus the guests set out on their round — the son in advance, excited and tremulous, the father anxious and watchful behind. They began in the usual way, with the old state-rooms and picture-gallery; and in a short time the party had half forgotten that there was anything unusual in the inspection. When, however, they were half-way down the gallery, Lindores stopped short with an air of wonder. "You have had it put back then?" he said. He was standing in front of the vacant space where Earl Robert's portrait ought to have been. "What is it?" they all cried, crowding upon him, ready for any marvel. But as there was nothing to be seen, the strangers smiled among themselves. "Yes, to be sure, there is nothing so suggestive as a vacant place," said a lady who was of the party. "Whose portrait ought to be there, Lord Lindores?"

He looked at his father, who made a slight assenting gesture, then shook his head drearily.

"Who put it there?" Lindores said, in a whisper.

"It is not there; but you and I see it," said Lord Gowrie, with a sigh.

Then the strangers perceived that something had moved the father and the son, and, notwithstanding their eager curiosity, obeyed the dictates of politeness, and dispersed into groups looking at the other pictures. Lindores set his teeth and clenched his hands. Fury was growing upon him — not the awe that filled his father's mind. "We will leave the rest of this to another time," he cried, turning to the others, almost fiercely. "Come, I will show you something more striking now." He made no further pretence of going systematically over the house. He turned and went straight upstairs, and along the corridor. "Are we going over the bed-rooms?" some one said. Lindores led the way straight to the old lumber-room, a strange place for such a gay party. The ladies drew their dresses about them. There was not room for half of them. Those who could get in began to handle the strange things that lay about, touching them with dainty fingers, exclaiming how dusty they were. The window was half blocked up by old armour and rusty weapons; but this did not hinder the full summer daylight from penetrating in a flood of light. Lindores went in with fiery determination on his face. He went straight to the wall, as if he would go through, then paused with a blank gaze. "Where is the door?" he said.

"You are forgetting yourself," said Lord Gowrie, speaking over the heads of the others. "Lindores! you know very well there never was any door there; the wall is very thick; you can see by the depth of the window. There is no door there."

The young man felt it over with his hand. The wall was smooth, and covered with the dust of ages. With a groan he turned away. At this moment a suppressed laugh, low, yet distinct, sounded close by him. "You laughed?" he said fiercely, to Ffarrington, striking his hand upon his shoulder.

"I — laughed! Nothing was farther from my thoughts," said his friend, who was curiously examing something that lay upon an old carved chair. "Look here! what a wonderful sword, cross-hilted! Is it an Andrea? What's the matter, Lindores?"

Lindores had seized it from his hands; he dashed it against the wall with a suppressed oath. The two or three people in the room stood aghast.

"Lindores!" his father said, in a tone of warning. The young man dropped the useless weapon with a groan. "Then God help us!" he said; "but I will find another way."

"There is a very interesting room close by," said Lord Gowrie, hastily — "this way! Lindores has been put out by — some changes that have been made without his knowledge," he said, calmly. "You must not mind him. He is disappointed. He is perhaps too much accustomed to have his own way."

But Lord Gowrie knew that no one believed him. He took them to the adjoining room, and told them some easy story of an apparition that was supposed to haunt it. "Have you ever seen it?" the guests said, pretending interest. "Not I; but we don't mind ghosts in this house," he answered, with a smile. And then they resumed their round of the old noble mystic house.

I cannot tell the reader what young Lindores has done to carry out his pledged word and redeem his family. It may not be known, perhaps, for another generation, and it will not be for me to write that concluding chapter; but when, in the ripeness of time, it can be narrated, no one will say that the mystery of Gowrie Castle has been a vulgar horror, though there are some who are disposed to think so now.

* * *

John Francis Campbell of Islay (1822-85) was one of the first and greatest collectors of the Gaelic tales which, like the Border ballads and legends, had been told and retold for centuries, usually by people with no book-learning but with strong memories and a gift for story-telling. Through one generation to another they gathered round the peat fire recounting, listening, remembering.

These stories were often of kings and queens, princes and princesses, whose kingdoms might be very small, hardly more than the state of a laird or chieftain. There was not so much about witchcraft as in the Border tales, but there was a great deal about fairy creatures of various sorts, of mermaids, of giants and sometimes a monster; but not the devil himself.

J.F. Campbell had a conventional education at Eton and Oxford, but before being sent away to school he was taught at home, learning the Gaelic and hearing some of the old tales from an aged servant. He travelled widely, in Lapland among other countries, and he held a Court appointment in the household of the Prince Consort. Did he ever tell any of those stories to the royal children in Buckingham Palace or

*at Windsor or Balmoral? Court life must have been
oppressively formal and it must have been a relief to escape
to his own country and wander from one island to another,
talking to the crofters and shepherds, the fishermen and the
old women of the Highlands and Western Isles, sitting with
them by their fires.*

He published four volumes of Popular Tales of the West
Highlands *with his own translation into English, and left a
quantity of manuscripts. These were taken up and translated
many years later by John McKay, with the help of other
Gaelic scholars as fellow-editors. The first volume of* More
West Highland Tales *appeared in 1940. John McKay died in
1942, leaving, as Campbell himself had done, more rich
material in manuscript. Again a group of scholars took up
the work, and the second volume was published in 1960.*

THE TALE OF THE QUEEN WHO SOUGHT A
DRINK FROM A CERTAIN WELL

There was before now, a queen who was sick, and she had
three daughters. Said she to the one who was eldest, "Go to
the well of true water, and bring to me a drink to heal me."

The daughter went, and she reached the well. A toad came
up to ask her if she would wed him, if she should get a drink
for her mother. "I will not wed thee, hideous creature! on
any account," said she. "Well then," said he, "thou shalt not
get the water."

She went away home, and her mother sent away her sister
that was nearest to her, to seek a drink of the water. She
reached the well; and the toad came up and asked her "if she
would marry him if she should get the water." "I won't
marry thee, hideous creature!" said she. "Thou shalt not get
the water, then," said he.

She went home, and her sister that was youngest went to
seek the water. When she reached the well the toad came up
as he used, and asked her "if she would marry him if she
should get the water." "If I have no other way to get healing
for my mother, I will marry thee," said she; and she got the
water, and she healed her mother.

They had betaken themselves to rest in the night when the
toad came to the door saying:-

"Gentle one, gentle one,
Rememberest thou
The little pledge
Thou gavest me
Beside the well,
My love, my love."

When he was ceaselessly saying this, the girl rose and took
him in, and put him behind the door, and she went to bed;
but she was not long laid down, when he began again saying,
everlastingly:-

"Gentle one, gentle one,
Rememberest thou
The little pledge
Thou gavest me
Beside the well,
My love, my love."

Then she got up and she put him under a noggin;* that
kept him quiet a while; but she was not long laid down when
he began again, saying:-

"Gentle one, gentle one,
Rememberest thou
The little pledge
Thou gavest me
Beside the well,
My love, my love."

She rose again, and she made him a little bed at the
fireside; but he was not pleased, and he began again saying,
"Gentle one, gentle one, rememberest thou the little pledge
thou gavest me beside the well, my love, my love." Then she
got up and made him a bed beside her own bed; but he was
without ceasing, saying, "Gentle one, gentle one,
rememberest thou the little pledge thou gavest me beside the
well, my love, my love." But she took no notice of his
complaining, till he said to her, "There is an old rusted glave†
behind thy bed, with which thou hadst better take off my
head, than be holding me longer in torture."

She took the glave and cut the head off him. When the

*a wooden cup
†a sword

steel touched him, he grew a handsome youth; and he gave many thanks to the young wife, who had been the means of putting off him the spells, under which he had endured for a long time. Then he got his kingdom, for he was a king: and he married the princess, and they were long alive and merry together.

from POPULAR TALES OF THE WEST HIGHLANDS

THE SMITH AND THE FAIRIES
Years ago there lived in Crossbrig a smith of the name of MacEachern. This man had an only child, a boy of about thirteen or fourteen years of age, cheerful, strong, and healthy. All of a sudden he fell ill; took to his bed and moped whole days away. No one could tell what was the matter with him, and the boy himself could not, or would not, tell how he felt. He was wasting away fast; getting thin, old, and yellow; and his father and all his friends were afraid that he would die.

At last one day, after the boy had been lying in this condition for a long time, getting neither better nor worse, always confined to bed, but with an extraordinary appetite, — one day, while sadly revolving these things, and standing idly at his forge, with no heart to work, the smith was agreeably surprised to see an old man, well known to him for his sagacity and knowledge of out-of-the-way things, walk into his workshop. Forthwith he told him the occurrence which had clouded his life.

The old man looked grave as he listened; and after sitting a long time pondering over all he had heard, gave his opinion thus — "It is not your son you have got. The boy has been carried away by the 'Daoine Sìth',* and they have left a *Sibhreach*† in his place." "Alas! and what then am I to do?" said the smith. "How am I ever to see my own son again?" "I will tell you how," answered the old man. "But, first, to make sure that it is not your own son you have got, take as many empty egg shells as you can get, go with them into the room, spread them out carefully before his sight, then

*'People of Peace' — a propitiatory name for fairies
†a fairy child

82

proceed to draw water with them, carrying them two and two in your hands as if they were a great weight, and arrange when full, with every sort of earnestness round the fire." The smith accordingly gathered as many broken egg-shells as he could get, went into the room, and proceeded to carry out all his instructions.

He had not been long at work before there arose from the bed a shout of laughter, and the voice of the seeming sick boy exclaimed, "I am now 800 years of age, and I have never seen the like of that before."

The smith returned and told the old man. "Well, now," said the sage to him, "did I not tell you that it was not your son you had: your son is in Brorra-cheill in a digh there (that is, a round green hill frequented by fairies). Get rid as soon as possible of this intruder, and I think I may promise you your son."

"You must light a very large and bright fire before the bed on which this stranger is lying. He will ask you 'What is the use of such a fire as that?' Answer him at once, 'You will see that presently!' and then seize him, and throw him into the middle of it. If it is your own son you have got, he will call out to save him; but if not, this thing will fly through the roof."

The smith again followed the old man's advice; kindled a large fire, answered the question put to him as he had been directed to do, and seizing the child flung him in without hesitation. The "Sibhreach" gave an awful yell, and sprung through the roof, where a hole was left to let the smoke out.

On a certain night the old man told him the green round hill, where the fairies kept the boy, would be open. And on that night the smith, having provided himself with a bible, a dirk, and a crowing cock, was to proceed to the hill. He would hear singing and dancing and much merriment going on, but he was to advance boldly; the bible he carried would be a certain safeguard to him against the danger from the fairies. On entering the hill he was to stick the dirk in the threshold, to prevent the hill from closing upon him; "and then," continued the old man, "on entering you will see a spacious apartment before you, beautifully clean, and there, standing far within, working at a forge, you will also see your own son. When you are questioned, say you come to seek him, and will not go without him."

Not long after this, the time came round, and the smith sallied forth, prepared as instructed. Sure enough as he approached the hill, there was a light where light was seldom seen before. Soon after a sound of piping, dancing, and joyous merriment reached the anxious father on the night wind.

Overcoming every impulse to fear, the smith approached the threshold steadily, stuck the dirk into it as directed, and entered. Protected by the bible he carried on his breast, the fairies could not touch him; but they asked him, with a good deal of displeasure, what he wanted there. He answered, "I want my son, whom I see down there, and I will not go without him."

Upon hearing this, the whole company before him gave a loud laugh, which wakened up the cock he carried dozing in his arms, who at once leaped up on his shoulders, clapped his wings lustily, and crowded loud and long.

The fairies, incensed, seized the smith and his son, and throwing them out of the hill, flung the dirk after them, "and in an instant a' was dark."

For a year and a day the boy never did a turn of work, and hardly ever spoke a word; but at last one day, sitting by his father and watching him finishing a sword he was making for some chief, and which he was very particular about, he suddenly exclaimed, "That is not the way to do it;" and taking the tools from his father's hands he set to work himself in his place, and soon fashioned a sword, the like of which was never seen in the country before.

From that day the young man wrought constantly with his father, and became the inventor of a peculiarly fine and well-tempered weapon, the making of which kept the two smiths, father and son, in constant employment, spread their fame far and wide, and gave them the means in abundance, as they before had the disposition to live content with all the world and very happily with one another.

from POPULAR TALES OF THE WEST HIGHLANDS

The fairies, incensed, threw them out of the hill

The theme of a mermaid captured by a mortal after she had laid off her tail or her fish-skin is frequent in poetry and legend, as is that of the seal-woman. The captive may fall in love with her captor, and settle down happily as wife and mother — as long as the skin is hidden. Finding it, usually by chance, awakens in her the irresistible call of the sea.

For sailors and fishermen to meet a mermaid at sea is unlucky and an omen of drowning; but a mermaid ashore can be friendly and helpful, showing gratitude and affection to men. This legend is from MORE WEST HIGHLAND TALES.

THE MERMAID

There was once a farmer called Otram, and one day he was passing through a wood near the sea when he saw, as he thought, seven seals moving towards the shore. He hid from them, and they came to land, and what were they but seven mermaids. They put off their fish skins and became seven beautiful young women; and now they set about washing themselves in the sea. Then Otram went and stole away the biggest of the skins and hid it. When the maidens came back to where the fish skins were, each of them found her own, all except the biggest maiden. She searched for her skin until she was exhausted. The others went off out to sea, but she remained there all alone, weeping and lamenting, seated on one of the stones of the shore, and naked. Otram came up to her and put his plaid round her and took her home with him. He found clothes for her, and she learned to do housework, and she was thrifty and industrious. Otram married her and she bore him children.

Long after that, one spring-time, Otram was out ploughing and his wife was out too, looking after things. When she came in, she said to her son, "Isn't it strange that your father is doing nothing about threshing that cornstack when very soon he will need the seed?' Her son replied, 'My father keeps a pretty thing in that stack: I have never seen anything so pretty.' She asked him what shape the thing had, and what colour; and the boy described its shape as best he could and said it was green in colour. She went into the garden where the stack was and scattered it all to pieces. The boy ran and told his father what had happened, and Otram hurried back to see his wife before she left him. But before he arrived, she had the fish skin on. He asked her to stay with him, but she would not. So he asked her to give him some counsel before she left him, and she counselled him to plough 'A furrow narrow, clean-cut, deep with the back of the sod beneath and scatter the seed though the wind were unfavourable; and good or bad the weather, sow the seed in March, and when the sun's warmth comes upon it it will grow up.'

And it is from the Mermaid's kind that the Clan —— are descended.

THE GRAY CAT

There was a King once, and he married, and his Queen bore him a son. The Queen died, and he married another Queen. The second Queen bore him another son and the two boys were growing up together. Every day the King went to the hunting hill, and his eldest son with him. The Iochlach Ùrlair* said to the Queen that she was truly foolish not to find a way of getting rid of the elder son, seeing that it was he who would inherit all his father's estate, whereas her own son would not have a scrap of it. 'You put this stuff in his cup when he comes home,' said she, 'and it will kill him.'

But who was listening to them but the younger brother, and when he heard his father and his brother coming he ran to meet them. The young boy told his brother not to take the drink his mother would give him. 'Because,' he said, 'the Iochlach Ùrlair told my mother to put something in it to kill you. But don't you tell, for fear my mother kills me.' When they sat down the youth took his own cup and gave it to the little dog that was in the house. The little dog died before he had finished drinking it. Not a word did the youth say, nor did he tell a thing, and the King was distressed when the little dog died.

Next day the King and his son went off to the hunting hill. After they had gone, the Iochlach Ùrlair came to the Queen. 'That was no use,' said she, 'but send him to me on an errand, and I will thrust a poisoned pin into him.' The younger boy

*domestic witch

87

was listening to them, and he ran to meet his father and brother when he saw them coming, and he told them every word that had passed between his mother and the Iochlach Ùrlair. 'If my mother sends you on an errand, don't go,' said the boy to his brother. The following day, after they had got up and had their breakfast, the Queen asked the youth to go on an errand to the Iochlach Ùrlair. When he went outside, he said to his brother, 'I will go away altogether, and you have the inheritance since it's to give you a clear field that they want to kill me.'

His brother was very grieved that the other was leaving. 'I will go in,' he said, 'to see if I can steal any money from my mother to bring you, for fear you are setting out with nothing.' 'I will not accept money that I could not get lawfully; it cannot do me any good,' said the elder brother; 'I would rather go away trusting to Fortune since I cannot obtain it in an honourable way.' The two brothers set off together, and a little way from the house they came to a green hillock. Here both of them began to weep, and then they took leave of each other. The younger remained face-downwards on the hillock and wept all day long. The elder brother went to the house of one of the King's foster-fathers, and arrived at nightfall. There was no one at home but his foster-mother, and she had a poor fire burning. 'Welcome, elder son of the King,' said she, 'it was easy to see that this is what it would come to at last.' She prepared a meal for him; she washed his feet with warm water and put him to bed; and she placed a slumber-straw under his head and his feet.

He slept without waking until daybreak and when he got up she made his breakfast. She gave him a pair of shoes and said to him: 'The shoes will bring you to the door of the cave where you are going. When you come to the door you will make the shoes face the way they know with their back to the way they do not know, and they will come to me here. Here are thirty silver shillings for you; it is all I have; take it with you. When you reach the cave and go in, you will see a great gray cat inside, and if the cat laughs at you, laugh back at her twice.' He told his foster-mother that he would do so; and taking his leave of her, he set off. The shoes brought him right up to the mouth of the cave, and when he arrived he

'Ho! ho! ho! the smell of a stranger is about the place'

made them face the way they knew with their back to the way they did not know, and they returned home.

He entered the cave and saw a great gray cat there. The cat laughed at him, and he laughed twice at the cat. 'Welcome to you, elder son of the King,' said the cat. 'Many a king's son and knight's son have come on this journey and have not returned home, and I fear that you will fare no better than they did. There is a great giant living here: every night he comes home, and though only a bird of the air enters, the giant notices it when he comes. But I will do my utmost for you, nevertheless.' The cat raised a great stone slab from off a pit on the far side of the fire, and a short time before the hour at which the giant used to come home she put him down into it, and placed the slab on the mouth of the pit and left him there.

They were not long thus when they heard a hubbub approaching and felt the earth quivering. Who was this but the Great Giant of Five Heads and Five Humps and Five Necks, with a withy of salmon in one hand and a withy of dead 'Old Women'* in the other. 'Ho! ho! ho! the smell of a stranger is about the place!' said the giant. 'It is only a little bird that came in, and I killed it and burnt it in the fire,' said the Gray Cat. 'Perhaps that's all it is,' said the giant. 'Hurry up and cook that fish for me.' She cooked the fish for him and he went to sleep on a bench. Not a snore he gave but seemed it would knock the house down. Next morning he ate the rest of the fish, and went off. When he had gone, the Gray Cat let the King's Son out of the pit. He asked the cat if there was any food there he might eat. There was not a bite, replied the cat, except some nasty fish. 'Not far from us is a town, and anything we need can be got there,' she said. "Here is some money,' said the King's Son, and he gave the cat part of the silver. Off she went to the town and bought wine and bread.

While the cat was away he decided to explore the cave to see what he could find. He saw a door, and it was locked. He peeped in through the keyhole and saw that every inch of the floor was covered with black pillar-stones. Then he went to

*probably black sea bream

another door and looked in through the keyhole. As far as he could see, he made out guns and swords and gentlemen's clothing. He went to another door; there he saw a beautiful young lady — a lovelier he had never seen — and she was dressed in white. She would spend some time weeping, and then she would comb her hair for a while. When he had inspected the three rooms and the cat had returned with what she had bought, he had a meal. 'If we keep on taking food in this way for a week until we become strong,' said the Gray Cat to the King's Son, 'this is what we will do: we will have a try at killing the Great Giant when he is sleeping.' 'Very good,' replied the King's Son. They continued to act in this way until the thirty shillings had gone. Every day when the cat was gone he would make for the room where the lady was, and he would spend the time looking through the keyhole until the cat returned. Every night when the giant came home he used to be very savage to the cat, insisting that there was a stranger in the house.

One night they determined to put an end to him. The giant had fallen into a heavy slumber, and, when he was sound asleep, the Gray Cat put on a great fire and put two roasting spits in the fire. The giant's snores were making the cave tremble. When the iron spits were white-hot the Gray Cat lifted the stone slab off the pit and let the King's Son out. He rose up, took one of the spits out of the fire, and thrust it through the giant's chest. The Gray Cat took out the other spit and, with what little strength she had, thrust it through another part of him. The giant rushed out shouting and crying. But what does he do but go through the door sideways and there the spits held him. The King's Son seized the giant's sword and said; 'Death is over your head! What is your ransom?' 'No little one,' replied the giant. 'There is a trunk full of gold and silver in one of the rooms in the cave.' 'That's mine!' said the King's Son. 'Death is over your head! What is your ransom?' 'I have a room full of black pillar-stones; they are none other than the children of kings and knights and dukes bound by enchantment. There is a magic wand in the room, and if you strike them with that wand they will resume their former shape. There is another room full of their clothes and weapons. What the wand will do for others it will do for the Gray Cat. She is a king's daughter who was bewitched, and I caught her. I was very good to her though ill has she repaid me in the end. But I have one possession better than all that — I have the daughter of the king of this very place. She was out swimming, and I caught her. I suppose you yourself will have that one.' Although the giant told him all that, the King's Son took off his heads with the sword.

The first thing he did after killing him was to go to the room where the lady was and let her out. Then they went to the room where the black pillar-stones and the magic wand were. He found the wand and gave the cat the first stroke with it. At once she became a fine, beautiful woman, about eighteen years old. Then he began striking the pillar-stones, and a king's son would leap up and a knight's son and a duke's son until the room was full of all those fine fellows. They dressed themselves in their own clothes in the other room. Then all the gold and silver was divided among them and the Gray Cat got her own good share of what was there. The young man and the King's daughter married, and the Gray Cat married one of the knights who had been in the room. When the weddings and everything else were over the King's Son thought he would go home where his father was. He took his wife with him, and along with them went treasure enough.

After the King's Son left his father's house, his father yearned for him, and everyone was very sorrowful because of his going. Every day his brother used to go to the hillock where he had parted from him to lament him; nor did anyone know what was ailing him. He was getting thin and wasting away. His father determined to follow him to find out where he was going. He followed him to the hillock and found him there, lying on his face weeping. 'You must tell me what's the matter with you,' said his father. The boy did not want to tell, but his father determined not to let him go until he had told. 'I'm afraid you will kill my mother if I tell,' said he. 'This is the hillock on which my darling brother parted from me. That night he went to my foster-father's house, and beyond that I have no trace of him.' The King went to his foster-father's house to see if he could find out

92

from his foster-mother what had happened to the youth. The foster-mother had nothing to tell him but that he had gone away. Then the King returned home and put the Iochlach Urlair to death. The Queen was so seized with shame that she took to her bed and did not live long.

When the King's Son and his father and brother met there was joy in plenty. The King's Son left the kingdom to his brother — he had abundance for himself. After he and his wife had spent some time with his father, they returned to their own kingdom. The king had now neither son nor daughter, except the younger son, and he married.

from MORE WEST HIGHLAND TALES

To know the name of a person was to have power over him or her. In many stories a mortal escapes through learning the secret name of a persecuting fairy or enchanter; in this story it brings power over the magic hounds.

Fairy tales are full of commands and prohibitions — do this; do not do that. There was a protective magic about keeping the fire in. The peat fire in a Hebridean or Highland home was smoored (covered with peat) at night, and stirred into fresh flame in the morning; never extinguished. There are many prayers and blessings for this ceremony of the hearth.

The jealous stepmother is well known in fairy tale. Usually her vindictiveness is against one person only, her stepson or stepdaughter. The flight of a brother and sister together is less frequent, and more unexpected still is the enmity of sister against brother.

THE THREE HOUNDS WITH THE GREEN STRINGS

There were once a King and a Queen who had a son and a daughter. The Queen died, and at the end of a number of years the King married another wife; but this last wife was very unkind to the children of the first. The children determined to go and seek their fortune; the King's Son took with him his bow and quiver, and the King's Daughter took with her three tawny-yellow crop-eared little pigs that she had. And off they went together, the two of them. As they were going across a moor, they came to a sheiling and went inside, and there they lived for a time. He used to go hunting while she stayed at home or near the bothy, preparing the venison and attending to the little pigs.

Early one morning he got up, and going out, saw a man coming towards the house, who had with him a fine hound with a green string about its neck. 'A fine hound you have there!' said the King's Son to him. 'Yes! will you buy it?' I have nothing to give you for it.' But the other, pointing to the young pigs, said, 'Give me one of those little pigs.' 'I can't do that: they are my sister's.' 'I will vouch for it that your sister will not mind.' And so the King's Son bartered one of his sister's little pigs for the hound. He went into the house with the hound and said to his sister, 'Is this not a fine hound that I have got here!' 'Yes,' she said; 'what did you give for that hound?' 'One of those little pigs of yours,' said he. 'Wild pigs and monsters come at you! You had no right to give my little pig away; it was none of yours.' 'I shall recover its value by hunting,' he replied. That day he went hunting, and the hound did exceeding well.

Next day he rose early and saw the same man he had seen the day before, and with him he had another hound with a green string round its neck. 'A fine hound you have there!' said the King's Son to him. 'Yes! will you buy it?' 'I have nothing to give you for it.' 'Will you not give me another one of the little pigs?' 'I can't do that; they are my sister's.' 'I will vouch for your sister.' And so the King's Son gave another of his sister's little pigs away in exchange for another hound. He went into the house with the hound and said to his sister, 'Is this not a fine hound that I have got?' 'Yes,' said she; 'what did you give for that hound?' 'One of those little pigs of yours.' 'Wild pigs and monsters come at you! You will ruin me, giving away my belongings in that fashion; you'll leave me destitute.' But he replied, 'There is no fear of not being able to buy it back, since I am with you; we shall get better hunting.' That day he went to the hill and the hounds hunted well for him; and how he praised them, when he came home!

Next day, having risen early, he saw the same man coming, and with him still another hound with a green string about its neck. 'Will you buy this hound?' 'I have nothing to give you for it.' 'Will you not give me another one of the little pigs?' 'I can't do that: they are my sister's.' 'I will vouch for your sister.' And so the King's Son bartered another of his sister's little pigs for another hound. On entering the house with the hound, he said to his sister, 'See what a fine hound I have got here.' 'Yes,' she said, 'what did you give for it?' 'Why, one of those little pigs of yours.' 'Wild pigs and monsters come at you! Now you have ruined me!' 'Don't worry, I shall always be with you; and I shall get plenty of game through having the three hounds.' He went hunting that day, and in a very short time he got plenty of venison. When he came home, he told his sister what a great hunting he had had, and in how short a time; but his sister would rather have had her three little pigs.

The next morning he went out and saw the same man again; and the man said to the King's Son, that if he regretted the bargain, he should have the little pigs back again in exchange for the hounds. The King's Son said that he had no regrets. Then said the other, 'You will be none the worse of knowing their names.' 'That is true,' said the King's Son. Then said the other, 'The name of the hound you had first is Knowledge; for he will always know where the quarry is, and besides he will give you warning if danger is near you. The name of the next hound you had from me is Swift; he will catch any quarry to which he gives chase, and if you were in any peril, he would be the first to come to your rescue. The name of the last hound you got is Weighty; he is strong, and good in a tussle, if you happened to be in distress.' And thus they parted. For a while the King's Son and Daughter stayed in the sheiling-hut and lived on venison.

One day as he was coming home from the hunting-hill, he sat down on a sunny little hillock that was above the house. Knowledge sighed heavily. 'Why do you sigh, Knowledge?' 'A Giant has bought the little pigs your sister had and he would like to get your hounds too. Unless you look after your sister, the Giant will steal her away.' 'How can she be kept safe?' Knowledge replied that he knew of no better way than to let her have everything she might want placed conveniently near her, so that she should not need to leave the house. Next day, before the King's Son went to the hunting-hill, he left everything his sister might want within reach and handy, and he ordered her to keep her hair combed and the house swept, and to see that she did not let the fire out, and that was all she had to do. He set out for the hill, but while his sister was combing her hair and sweeping the house, she let the fire go out. Away she went as quickly as ever she could, to see if she could find anywhere at all something to kindle the fire with.

While she was passing through a place strewn with rocks, she came across a sleeping giant. He had a fiery ember, and when he breathed out, he would blow the ember seven yards from him, and when he breathed in, he would suck the ember back to his mouth. For a while the King's Daughter stood looking at him, but at last she took the ember and ran off with it. The Giant woke up and noticed that the ember had been taken away. Up he got and ran after her, and caught hold of her just as she was going in at the door. He went inside with her, and she asked if she might keep the ember, no matter what she would have to give him in exchange for it. That was just what the Giant wanted; he told her he had bought the three little pigs she used to have, and that she might have them back again, and that they would protect her from every danger; that they would kill her brother, and that they would then get the three hounds, and be happy. They hatched the plot together, and the Giant placed a poisoned dart above the door, so that when her brother should be coming in the dart was to fall on him and kill him. And down underneath the cave they made a hole, and the Giant went down into the hole, and she covered him over.

When her brother was coming home from the hunting hill, he sat down on the sunny little hillock above the house. Knowledge sighed heavily. 'Why do you sigh, Knowledge?' 'Why, because your sister has let the fire out, and when she went to get something to kindle it with, she came across the

96

Giant who was blowing a fiery ember to and fro with his breath; she took the ember away with her, but the Giant followed her, and caught hold of her at the door. And they began to talk to each other, and they have made an agreement between them, and intend to kill you. The Giant has placed a poisoned dart above the door, which is to fall on you if you are the first to enter.' 'What then shall we do?' 'We shall do this: we shall send Swift in first, and if he goes in as fast as he can, he will have gone past before the dart has time to fall, and so only the tip of his tail will be taken off. The Giant is in a hole under the cave, at the side where the fire is. When you go in, put on the cauldron for the venison, and when it is ready, take out a bone, and throw it to us; then we will fight for the bone, and upset the cauldron; and we'll see if we can manage to scald the Giant to death.'

So Swift was sent in first. The poisoned dart did fall, but Swift had already got completely past, all but the tip of his tail, and the poisoned dart took off the tip. The dart itself sank seven yards into the earth. Then in came the King's Son and his two hounds. He put the cauldron for the venison on the fire. When the venison was ready, he took it off the fire and took out a bone which he threw to the hounds. The hounds fought over the bone and upset the cauldron, and the Giant gave a roar. The King's Son asked his sister, 'What was that roar?' 'The earth is opening because of the boiling water falling on it,' said she.

The next day when the King's Son and his hounds had gone to the hunting-hill, the Giant came up out of the hole, and after the King's Daughter had attended to him, he placed the poisoned dart above the door as it had been before. When the King's Son was coming home, the Giant went down again into the hole in the cave, and she covered him over. When he was coming down from the hill, the King's Son seated himself on the sunny hillock above the house. Knowledge sighed heavily. 'What makes you sigh, Knowledge?' 'Why,' said Knowledge, 'the Giant is not dead yet; he has put the poisoned dart above the door, as he did before, and he himself is in a hole under the floor, at the left side of the fire.' 'What shall we do?' 'We'll do as we did before,' said Knowledge; 'we'll send Swift in first; he will only lose a very little piece of the tip of his tail when the poisoned dart falls. We'll go in at his heels, and you put on the cauldron for the venison and when the venison is ready, take off the cauldron, and set it down just above the place where the Giant is. Then take out a bone and throw it to us. We will fight for the bone and upset the cauldron over the Giant, and see if we can kill him.'

So Swift was sent in first, and in he ran as swiftly as he could; the poisoned dart fell, but Swift had already got past, and so the poisoned dart did nothing but take off the tip of his tail. In at Swift's heels went the King's Son with his other two hounds. He did not let on that he knew anything about the Giant's being in the place, but he put the cauldron for the venison on the fire, and when the venison was ready, he took off the cauldron and set it on the ground just over where the Giant was. Then, taking a bone out of the cauldron, he threw it to the hounds, and instantly the hounds began to fight over it; and they upset the cauldron of boiling water on the Giant. The Giant gave a roar. The King's Son asked his sister, 'What was that roar?' 'It was only the earth opening because of the boiling water being poured on it,' she replied; and for the time being the matter was left at that.

The next day, when the King's Son had gone to the hill, his sister fetched up the Giant and attended to him by putting plasters on every spot that had been scalded. Again the Giant put the poisoned dart above the door, to fall upon the first one to come in. Then he went down into the hole again. When the King's Son arrived at the sunny hillock, he sat down there. Knowledge sighed heavily. 'Why do you sigh, Knowledge?' 'Why,' answered Knowledge, 'the Giant is not dead yet; he has put the poisoned dart above the door as he did before, and he himself is in a hole under the floor at the left side of the fire.' 'What shall we do?' 'We'll do as we did before, by sending Swift in first; and if he goes in as fast as he can, he will be past before the dart has time to fall, and only the top of his tail will be taken off. And when you come in, put on the cauldron for the venison, and when it is ready, take out a bone and throw it to us; we will fight for the bone and upset the cauldron; and we'll see if we can manage to scald the Giant to death.'

So Swift was sent in first, and in he ran as quickly as he could; the poisoned dart fell, but Swift had already got past, all but the tip of his tail, and the poisoned dart took off the tip. The King's Son and his two other hounds went in at Swift's heel. The King's Son gave no hint that he knew anything about the Giant's being there, but he put the cauldron for the venison on the fire, and when the venison was ready, he took the cauldron off and set it on the ground just over the place where the Giant was. Then taking a bone out of the cauldron he threw it to the hounds. The hounds began to fight over the bone; they upset the cauldron, but this time the Giant made no sound — he was scalded to death. The sister of the King's Son scowled, but she said not a word.

After a certain length of time, the King's Son was one day out hunting with his hounds when a mist came upon him, and he lost his way. He wandered about the hills, lost, and he travelled a long distance before he hit upon any house at all; but at last he came to one, the house of a gentleman, and he went up to the door. A handsome young woman came out and fetched him in, and he stayed some time in that place, and married the daughter of that gentleman.

In course of time, he thought he would go and see his sister and find out whether she was still alive; but he was going to leave his hounds at home along with his wife. His wife gave him three apples, and said to him, 'If any danger happens to come upon you, throw an apple behind you and shout, "Moorland and lakes behind me, and before me a clear road"; and if further danger comes upon you, throw another apple and shout, "Briers and thorns behind me, and before me a clear road"; and if yet more danger comes upon you, throw the third apple behind you, and shout, "Forest and moorland behind me, and before me a clear road."' Off he went, taking the three apples with him.

When he arrived at the sunny hillock above the house, he called out, 'Are you in, sister?' but she did not answer him. He called again but she gave no answer; then he called the third time, and she came out with three venomous little pigs she had got from the Giant. She set the three venomous little beasts at him, and he fled, but he threw an apple behind him and shouted, 'Moorland and lakes behind me, and before me a clear road,' and there grew up there a moorland and lakes through which the pigs could not go. But when the little beasts had come up to it, one of them said, 'If I had with me my big baler, my middling baler, and my little baler I'd not be long in making a road through this.' 'Go and fetch them,' said another pig. So off he went and got them, and they baled out the lake in a trice. Again they set off after him, but when they were coming very close to him, he threw another apple behind him and shouted, 'Briers and thorns behind me, and before me a clear road'; and the country behind grew so thick with briers and thorns that the little beasts had no means of thrusting themselves through. One of them spoke and said, 'If only I had with me my big sword, my middling sword, and my little sword, I'd not be long in driving a road through this.' 'Go and fetch them.' He went off and got them, and they cut a road through the briers and thorns, and they rushed after him again. When they were closing upon him, he threw the third apple behind him, and shouted, 'Moorland and forest behind me, and before me a clear road'; and there sprang up behind him such a moorland and forest that the little pigs were not able to thrust themselves through it, the trees were so close together and so thickly placed. One of the pigs said, 'If I had my big axe with me, my little axe, and my middling axe, I'd not be long in making a road through this.' 'You had better go and fetch them then,' said another; and the first one went off and got the axes, and they hacked a road through the forest, and away they rushed again after the King's Son. As they were closing upon him, he climbed high up into an oak tree. When they arrived at the tree, the little pigs began to dig it up by the roots. The King's Son whistled and Knowledge heard the whistle and said, 'Our master is in danger'; and the three hounds ran to succour their master. Swift was the first to arrive; and the three pigs set upon him and nearly killed him. But the next hound that came was Weighty; the three little pigs set upon him, but Weighty kept them at bay until at last Knowledge came; and then the three hounds killed the three little pigs.

The King's Son came home and he spent that night with

He climbed high up into an oak tree

his wife. The next day he went to see his sister. When he came to the sunny hillock above the house, he shouted, 'Are you in, sister?' She came out, and said, 'Yes, I am.' He asked her then if she was now willing to go with him; and she said she was. She went off with him, and they arrived at the house where he and his wife lived. The King's Son was head of the house and his wife mistress of the house, and the sister was there as if she were a servant, and it was she who used to make the beds.

But what had she in her possession but a poisoned dart that she had got from the Giant; and one night when she had made the bed, she put the poisoned dart into her brother's pillow, and when he went to rest, the poisoned dart went into his head. He fainted away in a swoon as though he were dead, and remained in that state for three days, and then they buried him. But over the grave where he was buried his three hounds set to work to scratch. Then came his wife, and she said to them, 'What is the good of your scratching there? He is dead, and we cannot bring him to life again.' But Knowledge said, 'If you would only take the earth away, I would try to bring him to life.' So then the earth was taken away, and Knowledge took the poisoned dart out of the back of his head and he came to life again. He went home and made a great fire of green oak, and when the fire was burning well, he threw his sister on it. And the man who told me the story said that he left the man, his wife, and his hounds together in love, esteem, and playful affection.

from MORE WEST HIGHLAND TALES

THE SHARP GREY SHEEP

There was a king and a queen, and they had a daughter, and the queen found death, and the king married another. And the last queen was bad to the daughter of the first queen, and she used to beat her and put her out of the door. She sent her to herd the sheep, and was not giving her what should suffice her. And there was a sharp horned grey sheep in the flock that was coming with meat to her.

The queen was taking wonder that she was keeping alive and that she was not getting meat enough from herself, and she told it to the henwife. The henwife thought that she would send her own daughter to watch how she was getting meat, and the bald scabby girl, the henwife's daughter, went to herd the sheep with the queen's daughter. The sheep would not come to her so long as the bald scabby girl was there, and the bald scabby girl was staying all the day with her. The queen's daughter was longing for her meat and she said — "Set they head on my knee and I will dress thy hair." And the bald scabby girl set her head on the knee of the queen's daughter, and she slept.

The sheep came with meat to the queen's daughter, but the eye that was in the back of the head of the bald black-skinned girl, the henwife's daughter, was open, and she saw all that went on, and when she awoke she went home and told it to her mother, and the henwife told it to the queen, and when the queen understood how the girl was getting meat, nothing at all would serve her but that the sheep should be killed.

The sheep came to the queen's daughter and said to her —

"They are going to kill me, but steal thou my skin and gather my bones and roll them in my skin, and I will come alive again, and I will come to thee again."

The sheep was killed, and the queen's daughter stole her skin, and she gathered her bones and her hoofs and she rolled them in the skin; but she forgot the little hoofs. The sheep came alive again, but she was lame. She came to the king's daughter with a halting step, and she said, "Thou didst as I desired thee, but thou hast forgotten the little hoofs."

And she was keeping her in meat after that.

There was a young prince who was hunting and coming often past her, and he saw how pretty she was, and he asked, "Who's she?" And they told him, and he took love for her, and he was often coming the way; but the bald black-skinned girl, the henwife's daughter, took notice of him, and she told it to her mother, and the henwife told it to the queen.

The queen was wishful to get knowledge what man it was, and the henwife sought till she found out who he was, and she told the queen. When the queen heard who it was she was wishful to send her own daughter in his way, and she brought in the first queen's daughter, and she sent her own daughter to herd in her place, and she was making the daughter of the first queen do the cooking and every service about the house.

The first queen's daughter was out a turn, and the prince met her, and he gave her a pair of golden shoes. And he was wishful to see her at the sermon, but her muime* would not let her go there.

But when the rest would go she would make ready, and she would go after them, and she would sit where he might see her, but she would rise and go before the people would scatter, and she would be at the house and everything in order before her muime* would come. But the third time she was there the prince was wishful to go with her, and he sat near to the door, and when she went he was keeping an eye on her, and he rose and went after her. She was running home, and she lost one of her shoes in the mud; and he got the shoe, and because he could not see her he said that the one who had the foot that would fit the shoe was the wife that would be his.

The queen was wishful that the shoe would fit her own daughter, and she put the daughter of the first queen in hiding, so that she should not be seen till she should try if the shoe should fit her own daughter.

When the prince came to try the shoe on her, her foot was too big, but she was very anxious that the shoe should fit her, and she spoke to the henwife about it. The henwife cut the points of her toes off that the shoe might fit her, and the shoe went on her when the points of the toes were cut.

When the wedding- day came the daughter of the first queen was set in hiding in a nook that was behind the fire.

When the people were all gathered together, a bird came to the window, and he cried —

"The blood's in the shoe, and the pretty foot's in the nook at the back of the fire."

One of them said, "What is that creature saying?" And the queen said — "It's no matter what that creature is saying; it is but a nasty, beaky, lying creature." The bird came again to

*stepmother

the window; and the third time he came, the prince said —
"We will go and see what he is saying."

And he rose and he went out, and the bird cried —

"The blood's in the shoe, and the pretty foot's in the nook
that is at the back of the fire."

He returned in, and he ordered the nook at the back of the
fire to be searched. And they searched it, and they found the
first queen's daughter there, and the golden shoe on the one
foot. They cleaned the blood out of the other shoe, and they
tried it on her, and the shoe fitted her, and its like was on the
other foot. The prince left the daughter of the last queen,
and he married the daughter of the first queen, and he took
her from them with him, and she was rich and lucky after
that.

from POPULAR TALES OF THE WEST HIGHLANDS

*J.F. Campbell's work was also continued by a fellow
clansman, Lord Archibald Campbell (1846-1913), son of the
eighth Duke of Argyll. He was general editor, with the
collaboration of a number of Gaelic scholars, of a new
collection:* Waifs and Strays of Celtic Tradition, *in five
volumes. Among those delightful waifs and strays are:* The
Smith's Rock in the Isle of Skye; The Farmer of Liddesdale;
and The Fairies' Hill.

THE SMITH'S ROCK IN THE ISLE OF SKYE

There was a report that the Fians (Fingalians) were asleep
in this Rock, and that if anyone would enter it and blow the
Wooden-Crier (Whistle), which lay beside Finn, three times,
they would rise up alive and well as they formerly were.

A Smith who lived in the island heard the report, and
resolved that he would attempt to enter the Rock. He
reached the place where it was; and, having formed a good
idea of the key-hole, he returned to the smithy, and made a
key which fitted the hole. He then went back to the Rock,
and, as soon as he turned the key in the hole, the door
opened, and he saw a very great and wide place before him,

He blew it with all his might

and exceedingly big men lying on the floor. One man, bigger than the rest, was lying in their midst, having a large hollow baton of wood lying beside him.

He thought that this was the Wooden-Crier. But it was so large that he was afraid that he could not lift it, much less blow it. He stood for a time looking at it, but he at last said to himself that, as he came so far, he would try at any rate. He laid hold of the Wooden-Crier, and with difficulty raised its end up to his mouth. He blew it with all his might, and so loud was the sound it produced that he thought the Rock and all that was over it came down on the top of him. The huge unwieldy men who lay on the floor shook from the tops of their heads to the soles of their feet. He gave another blast on the Wooden-Crier, and with one spring they turned on their elbows. Their fingers were like the prongs of wooden grapes, and their arms like beams of bog-oak. Their size and the terrible appearance they had put him in such fear that he threw the Wooden-Crier from him, and sprang out. They were then crying after him, "Worse have you left us than as you found us, worse have you left us than as you found us." But he looked not behind him until he got outside and shut the door. He then drew the key out of the hole, and threw it out into the lake which is near the Rock, and which is called to this day the Lake of the Smith's Rock.

THE FARMER OF LIDDESDALE

There was in Liddesdale (in Morven) a Farmer who suffered great loss within the space of one year. In the first place, his wife and children died, and shortly after their death the Ploughman left him. The hiring-markets were then over, and there was no way of getting another ploughman in place of the one that left. When Spring came his neighbours began ploughing; but he had not a man to hold the plough, and he knew not what he should do. The time was passing, and he was therefore losing patience. At last he said to himself, in a fit of passion, that he would engage the first man that came his way, whoever he should be.

Shortly after that a man came to the house. The Farmer met him at the door, and asked him whither was he going, or

what was he seeking? He answered that he was a Ploughman, and that he wanted an engagement. "I want a ploughman, and if we agree about the wages, I will engage thee. What dost thou ask from this day to the day when the crop will be gathered in?" "Only as much of the corn when it shall be dry as I can carry with me in one burden-withe."*
"Thou shalt get that," said the Farmer, and they agreed.

Next morning the Farmer went out with the Ploughman, and showed him the fields which he had to plough. Before they returned, the Ploughman went to the wood, and having cut three stakes, came back with them, and placed one of them at the head of each one of the fields. After he had done that he said to the Farmer, "I will do the work now alone, and the ploughing need no longer give thee anxiety."

Having said this, he went home, and remained idle all that day. The next day came, but he remained idle as on the day before. After he had spent a good while in that manner, the Farmer said to him that it was time for him to begin work now, because the spring was passing away, and the neighbours had half their work finished. He replied, "Oh, our land is not ready yet." "How dost thou think that?" "Oh, I know it by the stakes."

If the delay of the Ploughman made the Farmer wonder, this answer made him wonder more. He resolved that he would keep his eye on him, and see what he was doing.

The Farmer rose early next morning, and saw the Ploughman going to the first field. When he reached the field, he pulled the stake at its end out of the ground, and put it to his nose. He shook his head and put the stake back in the ground. He then left the first field and went to the rest. He tried the stakes, shook his head, and returned home. In the dusk he went out the second time to the fields, tried the stakes, shook his head, and after putting them again in the ground, went home. Next morning he went out to the fields the third time. When he reached the first stake he pulled it out of the ground and put it to his nose as he did on the foregoing days. But no sooner had he done that than he

*a *withe* is a willow branch. A *burden-withe* is a band of willows used as a pack.

108

He pulled the stake out of the ground

threw the stake from him, and stretched away for the houses with all his might.

He got the horses, and withes, and the plough, and when he reached the end of the first field with them, he thrust the plough into the ground, and cried:

"My horses and my leather-traces, and mettlesome lads,
The earth is coming up!"

He then began ploughing, kept at it all day at a terrible rate, and before the sun went down that night there was not a palm-breadth of the three fields which he had not ploughed, sowed, and harrowed. When the Farmer saw this he was exceedingly well pleased, for he had his work finished as soon as his neighbours.

The Ploughman was quick and ready to do everything that he was told, and so he and the Farmer agreed well until the harvest came. But on a certain day when the reaping was over, the Farmer said to him that he thought the corn was dry enough for putting in. The Ploughman tried a sheaf or two, and answered that it was not dry yet. But shortly after that day he said that it was now ready. "If it is," said the Farmer, "we better begin putting it in." "We will not until I get my share out of it first," said the Ploughman. He then went off to the wood, and in a short time returned, having in his hand a withe scraped and twisted. He stretched the withe on the field, and began to put the corn in it. He continued putting sheaf after sheaf in the withe until he had taken almost all the sheaves that were on the field. The Farmer asked of him what he meant? "Thou didst promise me as wages as much corn as I could carry with me in one burden-withe, and here I have it now," said the Ploughman, as he was shutting the withe.

The Farmer saw that he would be ruined by the Ploughman, and therefore said:

"'Twas in the Màrt I sowed,*
'Twas in the Màrt I baked,
'Twas in the Màrt I harrowed.

*The Màrt is the right time or season for any work: spring for sowing; autumn for baking from new-ground meal and for reaping

110

Thou who hast ordained the three Màrts,
Let not my share go in one burden-withe."

Instantly the withe broke, and it made a loud report, which
echo answered from every rock far and near. Then the corn
spread over the field, and the Ploughman went away in a
white mist in the skies, and was seen no more.

THE FAIRIES' HILL

There is a green hill above Kintraw, known as the Fairies'
Hill, of which the following story is told.

Many years ago, the wife of the farmer at Kintraw fell ill
and died, leaving two or three young children. The Sunday
after the funeral the farmer and his servants went to church,
leaving the children at home in charge of the eldest, a girl of
about ten years of age. On the farmer's return the children
told him their mother had been to see them, and had combed
their hair and dressed them. As they still persisted in their
statement after being remonstrated with, they were
punished for telling what was not true. The following
Sunday the same thing occurred again. The father now told
the children, if their mother came again, they were to inquire
of her why she came. Next Sunday, when she reappeared,
the eldest child put her father's question to her, when the
mother told them she had been carried off by the "Good
People", and could only get away for an hour or two on
Sundays, and should her coffin be opened it would be found
to contain only a withered leaf. The farmer, much
perplexed, went to the minister for advice, who scoffed at
the idea of any supernatural connection with the children's
story, ridiculed the existence of "Good People". and would
not allow the coffin to be opened. The matter was therefore
allowed to rest. But, some little time after, the minister, who
had gone to Lochgilphead for the day, was found lying dead
near the Fairies' Hill, a victim, many people thought, to the
indignation of the Fairy world he had laughed at.

One of Lord Archibald Campbell's fellow editors was the Reverend John Gregorson Campbell (1836-1891), the minister of the islands of Coll and Tiree, and a friend and contemporary of J.F. Campbell of Islay. He too was a Gaelic scholar, at home with his people, and a good listener. Besides his volume in the series of Waifs and Strays of Celtic Tradition, *he published two of his own on witchcraft, superstition and second sight. From* Witchcraft and Second Sight in the Scottish Highlands *comes the gruesome tale of* The Grey Paw.

In the big church of Beauly, mysterious and unearthly sights and sounds were seen and heard at night, and none who went to watch the churchyard or burial-places within the church ever came back alive. A courageous tailor made light of the matter and laid a wager that he would go any night, and sew a pair of hose in the haunted church. He went and began his task. The light of the full moon streamed in through the windows, and at first all was silent and natural. At the dead hour of midnight, however, a big ghastly head emerged from a tomb and said, "Look at the old grey cow that is without food, tailor." The tailor answered, "I see that and I sew this," and soon found that while he spoke the ghost was stationary, but when he drew breath it rose higher. The neck emerged and said, "A lŏng grizzled weasand* that is without food, tailor." The tailor went on with his work in fear, but answered, "I see it, my son, I see it, my son, I see that and I sew this just now." This he said drawling out his words to their utmost length. At last his voice failed and he inhaled a long breath. The ghost rose higher and said, "A long grey arm that is without flesh or food, tailor." The trembling tailor went on with his work and answered, "I see it, my son, I see it, my son; I see that and I sew this just now." Next breath the thigh came up and the ghastly apparition said, "A long, crooked shank that is without meat, tailor." "I see it, my son, I see it, my son; I see that and I sew this just now." The long foodless and fleshless arm was now stretched in the direction of the tailor. "A long

*gullet

112

The trembling tailor went on with his work

grey paw without blood or flesh, or muscles, or meat tailor."
The tailor was near done with his work and answered, "I see
it, my son, I see it, my son; I see that and I sew this just now,"
while with a trembling heart he proceeded with his work. At
last he had to draw breath, and the ghost, spreading out its
long and bony fingers and clutching the air in front of him,
said. "A big grey claw that is without meat, tailor." At that
moment the last stitch was put in the hose, and the tailor
gave one spring of horror to the door. The claw stuck at him
and the point of the fingers caught him by the bottom
against the door-post and took away the piece. The mark of
the hand remains on the door to this day. The tailor's flesh
shook and quivered with terror, and he could cut grass with
his haunches as he flew home.

* * *

*John Buchan (1875-1940) was the true heir and successor of
Scott, of whom he wrote an excellent biography, and Hogg.
A Borderer by descent if not by birthplace (he was born in
Perth where his father was a Free Church minister), he loved
the hills and valleys of Tweedside, and he never forgot the
inner country there, which Scott and Hogg knew well; the
place of magic and witchcraft.*

In his autobiography, Memory-Hold-the-Door, *he
recalls his love of tales and legends, nourished by his father's
library. Two books had a special influence. One (to be
expected on manse bookshelves) was* The Pilgrim's
Progress; *the other was the old tale of* The Red Etin of
Ireland. *There were some of the Norse myths too — all of
which went to the making of a story-teller.*

*Buchan was a good scholar and very much a man of
affairs. From Glasgow University he went to Oxford, where
he began to write, then to South Africa with Lord Milner.
Writing was a vocation among many other activities. He
went into publishing with Nelson's, became a Member of
Parliament, and finally was appointed Governor General of
Canada.*

*As an author he was for years a best-seller, chiefly
through his saga of the adventures of Richard Hannay, but
he also wrote historical novels, biography, and poetry. And,*

*what concerns us here, he wrote of that other borderland
country of magic and witchery sometimes not far removed
from the diabolic.* The Watcher by the Threshold *is one
collection of such tales, of which the most moving is* The
Outgoing of the Tide.

In one of his best novels, Witch Wood, *he takes us into the
dark background of seventeenth-century Scotland. His
hero, David Sempill, minister of a Border parish, discovers
the dreadful cult of Satanism practised, not by the
disreputably among his parishioners, but by the apparently
strict and godly.*

Suddenly he came into a broad glade over which the
moonshine flowed like a tide. It was all of soft mossy green,
without pebble or bush to break its carpet, and in the centre
stood a thing like an altar.

At first he thought it was only a boulder dropped from the
hill. But as he neared it he saw that it was human handiwork.
Masons centuries ago had wrought on it, for it was roughly
squared, and firmly founded on a pediment. Weather had
battered it, and one corner of the top had been broken by
some old storm, but it still stood four-square to the seasons.
One side was very clear in the moon, and on it David
thought he could detect a half-obliterated legend. He knelt
down, and though the lower part was obscured beyond
hope, the upper letters stood out plain. I. O. M. — he read:
"Jovi Optimo Maximo." This uncouth thing had once been
an altar.

He tiptoed away from it with a sudden sense of awe.
Others had known this wood — mailed Romans clanking up
the long roads from the south, white-robed priests who had
once sacrificed here to their dead gods. He was scholar
enough to feel the magic of this sudden window opened into
the past. But there was that in the discovery which
disquieted as well as charmed him. The mysteries of the
heathen had been here, and he felt the simplicity of the
woodland violated and its peace ravished. Once there had
been wild tongues in the air, and he almost seemed to hear
their echo.

He hurried off into the dark undergrowth . . . But now his

mood had changed. He felt fatigue, his eyes were drowsy, and he thought of the anxious Isobel sitting up for him. He realized that this was the night of Rood-Mass — pagan and papistical folly, but his reason could not altogether curb his fancy. The old folk said — folly, no doubt, but still —— He had an overpowering desire to be safe in his bed at the manse. He would retrace his steps and strike the road from Reiverslaw. That would mean going west, and after a moment's puzzling he started to run in what he thought the right direction.

The Wood, or his own mind, had changed. The moonlight was no longer gracious and kind, but like the dead-fires which the old folk said burned in the kirkyard. Confusion on the old folk, for their tales were making him a bairn again! . . . But what now broke the stillness? for it seemed as if there were veritably tongues in the air — not honest things like birds and winds, but tongues. The place was still silent so far as earthly sounds went — he realized that, when he stopped to listen — but nevertheless he had an impression of movement everywhere, of rustling — yes, and of tongues.

Fortune was against him, for he reached a glade and saw that it was the one which he had left and which he thought he had avoided . . . There was a change in it, for the altar in the centre was draped. At first he thought it only a freak of moonlight, till he forced himself to go nearer. Then he saw that it was a coarse white linen cloth, such as was used in the kirk at the seasons of sacrament.

The discovery affected him with a spasm of blind terror. All the tales of the Wood, all the shrinking he had once felt for it, rushed back on his mind. For the moment he was an infant again, lost and fluttering, assailed by the shapeless phantoms of the dark. He fled from the place as if from something accursed.

Uphill he ran, for he felt that safety was in the hills and that soon he might come to the clear spaces of the heather. But a wall of crag forced him back, and he ran as he thought westward towards the oaks and hazels, for there he deemed he would be free of the magic of the pines. He did not run wildly, but softly and furtively, keeping to the moss and the darker places, and avoiding any crackling of twigs, for he

116

felt as if the Wood were full of watchers. At the back of his head was a stinging sense of shame — that he, a grown man and a minister of God, should be in such a pit of terror. But his instinct was stronger than his reason. He felt his heart crowding into his throat, and his legs so weak and uncontrollable that they seemed to be separate from his body. The boughs of the undergrowth whipped his face, and he knew that his cheeks were wet with blood, though he felt no pain.

The trees thinned and he saw light ahead — surely it was the glen which marked the division between pine and hazel. He quickened his speed, and the curtain of his fear lifted ever so little. He heard sounds now — was it the wind which he had left on the hilltops? There was a piping note in it, something high and clear and shrill — and yet the Wood had been so airless that his body was damp with sweat. Now he was very near air and sanctuary.

His heart seemed to stop, and his legs wavered so that he sunk on his knees. For he was looking again on the accursed glade.

It was no longer empty. The draped altar was hidden by figures — human or infernal — moving round it in a slow dance. Beyond this circle sat another who played on some instrument. The moss stilled the noise of movement, and the only sound was the high, mad piping.

A film cleared from his eyes, and something lost came back to him — manhood, conscience, courage. Awe still held him, but it was being overmastered by a human repulsion and anger. For as he watched the dance he saw that the figures were indeed human, men and women both — the women half-naked, but the men with strange headpieces like animals. What he had taken for demons from the Pit were masked mortals — one with the snout of a pig, one with a goat's horns, and the piper a gaping black hound . . . As they passed, the altar was for a moment uncovered, and he saw that food and drink were set on it for some infernal sacrament.

The dance was slow and curiously arranged, for each woman was held close from behind by her partner. And they danced widdershins, against the sun. To one accustomed to

117

the open movement of country jigs and reels the thing seemed the uttermost evil — the grinning masks, the white tranced female faces, the obscene postures, above all that witch-music as horrid as a moan of terror.

David, a great anger gathering in his heart, was on his feet now, and as he rose the piping changed. Its slow measure became a crazy lilt, quick and furious. The piper was capering; the dancers, still going widdershins, swung round and leaped forward, flinging their limbs as in some demented reel . . . There were old women there, for he saw grey hair flying. And now came human cries to add to the din of the pipe — a crying and a sighing wrung out of maddened bodies.

To David it seemed a vision of the lost in Hell. The fury of an Israelitish prophet came upon him. He strode into the glade. Devils or no, he would put an end to this convention of the damned.

"In the name of God," he cried, "I forbid you. If you are mortal, I summon you to repent — if you are demons, I command you to return to him that sent you."

He had a great voice, but in that company there were no ears to hear. The pipe screeched and the dance went on.

Then the minister of Woodilee also went mad. A passion such as he had never known stiffened every nerve and sinew. He flung himself into the throng, into that reek of unclean bestial pelts and sweating bodies. He reached the altar, seized the cloth on it, and swept it and its contents to the ground. Then he broke out of the circle and made for the capering piper, who seemed to him the chief of the orgiasts.

In his flight through the wood David had lost his staff, and had as weapon but his two hands. "Aroynt you, Sathanas," he cried, snatched the pipe from the dog-faced figure, and shivered it on his masked head.

With the pause in the music the dance stopped suddenly, and in an instant the whole flock were on him like a weasel pack. He saw long-nailed claws stretched towards his face, he saw blank eyes suddenly fire into a lust of hate. But he had a second's start of them, and that second he gave to the piper. The man — for the thing was clearly human — had dealt a mighty buffet at his assailant's face, which missed it,

The whole flock were on him like a weazel pack

and struck the point of the shoulder. David was whirled round, but, being young and nimble, he slipped in under the other's guard, and had his hands on the hound-mask. The man was very powerful, but the minister's knee was in his groin, and he toppled over, while David tore the covering of wood and skin from his head. It crumpled under his violent clutch like a wasps' nest, and he had a glimpse of red hair and a mottled face.

A glimpse and no more. For by this time the press was on him and fingers were at his throat, choking out his senses.

Neil Gunn (1891-1974) was as direct a descendant and heir of the Highland story-tellers as Buchan was of the Border tradition. He was a man of the north-east, born in Dunbeath, Caithness, the region of which he writes most. He went to the local school, then for two years stayed with a married sister in Galloway. Much of his boyhood has been recorded directly in his Atom of Delight; *less directly and even more entrancingly in* Young Art and Old Hector, *which tells of the friendship between a tough small boy and a wise old man.*

Neil Gunn entered the Civil Service, but retired, in 1937, to absorb himself in writing — with rich results. Like Buchan he cherished his heritage: young Art hears much lore from old Hector and absorbs more than he realises. The tradition of story-telling is still strong, and the story told to Art by old Martha can be found among J.F. Campbell's Popular Tales of the West Highlands. *It is retold here as it has been told for centuries by peat fires in little smoky houses, or wherever folk have gathered together.*

MACHINERY
Happening to turn his eyes, Donul saw Martha with the shaking head going towards the mill through the dusk of the evening. "Now run you home," he said to his little brother Art, "and if they ask you, say I'll be home in a short while."

But Art would not run home, and from being kind

Martha with the shaking head was going towards the mill

Donul's voice grew harsh and angry. "I'll wallop the face off you if you don't go this minute."

Art fell with the push he got, and Donul ran towards the mill. Yelling loudly, Art, from his knees and his little hands, got to his feet and ran after Donul as hard as he could.

Donul saw Martha lift up her head. Moving there across the land she was like a fearsome old scarecrow. He stopped, and Art stopped short of him. Donul picked up a stone and said in a low fierce voice to Art: "If you don't go home this minute I'll knock your brain out."

Art sobbed in little sniffs and picked his breast, his head down, but whenever Donul went on Art followed him. Martha had now gone into the mill. Donul looked around to make sure that no-one would see the terrible thing he was going to do to his brother. There was no-one, so he nodded grimly and strode back to Art. Art held his yell ready. "Will you go home?" asked Donul like thunder and lightning. Art did not answer, his eyes gleaming up once. "Will you go home?" cried Donul, and gripped his brother by the back of the neck.

Art yelled.

"Come on!" cried Donul, and began to drag him home. But Art would not be dragged. "So you won't come home with me?" demanded Donul in wild triumph. "You won't come home?" And he walloped Art. Art yelled as if he were being murdered, and though Donul now knew himself to be in the right, he crouched under that sound, looking over his shoulders. Art was sobbing, curled up on the ground. It's not one thing an elder brother has to bear. "Go on, keep crying," he said to Art; "keep crying, you mother's baby!" Then he jerked his brother into sitting up. "Stop it and wipe your nose, you little fool." Art heard the inner change in his brother's voice and tried to stop crying. Donul wiped his eyes for him roughly. "Come on," said Donul, taking Art by the hand, and they went towards the mill.

Art had cried so much and been obstinate because he was afraid to go to the mill and therefore wanted to go desperately. He had heard in his time many strange stories about the mill, and about more mills than this one. For there was a thing in the mill called machinery and it went round and round, with teeth on the edges of its wheels, and though one wheel was standing up and the next one lying down, their teeth would bite into one another like Art's own teeth, and woe and betide anything that came between them then. Donul had said they would bite your whole head off and hardly notice it; your whole hand, right off. And if the iron teeth caught your sleeve they would "drag you in".

Art had seen the water-wheel outside going splash! splash! and had once drawn near to the edge of the black hole down through which the flood disappeared with such rumbling, gushing sounds that the earth under his feet had quaked. But he had never gone near it thereafter, because Kennie-the-kiln had appeared and said in a terrible voice that if ever he found Art about the mill again he would throw him into the black hole.

But the most awful thing about the mill was the going round and round. Three thieves had once broken into a mill, but the miller was clever, because he had shut the doors and sent the mill round and round. The thieves grew dizzy, and then they couldn't stand, and then they fell, and there they lay like ones dead and so were easily captured. And there was one story of a miller in the dead of night and of a man who came to murder him, but the man didn't murder the miller and instead got murdered himself. It was such a story as his mother wouldn't allow to be told before Art, but one day when Donul was wanting Art to do something for him, Art got the story out of Donul.

The mill was high, higher than three houses, and had cocked angles on it and little windows. There were hens round it and a water pool near the wheel where ducks floated. Men came whom Art didn't know, from places to which Art had never been, with sacks of oats in a cart, and backed in the cart below a door which was not like any ordinary door on the ground but high up in the wall. It was said that the machinery pulled the sacks up by the chain. And how could the machinery pull the sacks up unless the machinery knew how to do it? Darkly Art suspected that this machinery had more in it than men who laughed at him believed. They had better look out or one day it would catch and drag them in. He would have liked to ask Donul if it might, but his thought was not too settled yet, and in any case, there were now no hens and no ducks and no carts, and — the mill was silent.

They passed under the little wooden bridge that spanned the cavern to the top floor and approached the vast red-smouldering heap of husks which Kennie had thrown from the kiln fire. As they entered at the door, Donul shoved Art behind him, and Art followed like Donul's shadow.

It would have been dark inside but for the kiln fire, which put red gleams on the faces of bearded men. Many of them were laughing and their voices threw dancing shadows. They were so taken up pulling fun out of old Martha that they did not notice the boys come in. Donul sat down against the wall and Art crouched by him. Two other boys, as old as Donul, saw Art, and smiled to him in subdued greeting, but said nothing. Then the four of them looked at Martha, who was answering the men, her head nodding at a great rate. She sat on a full sack, with a loose neck coming up out of dark rounded shoulders, like the plucked throat of an old raven. Her head kept swinging back and fore on a well-oiled swivel. In this movement the boys found a terrifying fascination. "Hush!" said Donul softly to Art, who had said nothing.

Art might not have been able to understand some of the grown-up jests even if he had been able to listen. But words themselves had become queer sounds now. This was a ceilidh in a weird place. The shadows were peaked gnomes, very swift. In the bearded faces was a laughing glancing that was not in them at home.

"You can tie him up, as you did last time, and blindfold him," said Martha, "and you can say Smell that and Taste that," and she tried in her mirth to shake her head sideways, and so induced a complicated motion awesome to behold.

"We made the gauger so drunk that he was frightened to report us anyway, didn't we, Martha?"

"No, oh no," said Martha, whirring as if about to strike a long hour. "He had only smelt and tasted and drunk himself under, but he had seen nothing on top, so what could he say he had seen?"

They liked their own joke to be explained to them by

Martha and laughed with great pleasure, throwing their heads up, and some of them even nodding in sympathy with Martha, who was now nodding at a great rate.

"Well, if we made a good drop that time, the gauger couldn't complain but that we gave him his share of it. Eh, Martha?"

"There is a difference," answered Martha, "between him who has the boil and him who squeezes it."

Because the others were laughing, little Art now ventured on a smile himself. And soon the words he heard were more like the words he knew. And presently they asked Martha to tell a story, for it was a good way to put in the time while the grain was drying. "Hush!" said Donul to Art who had no thought of saying anything.

When Martha asked what story they would like, a man answered, "The Girl and the Dead Man."

"I have told that one many's the time," said Martha.

"It's none the worse for that," declared the man.

There was once a poor woman and she had three daughters (Martha began). Up got the eldest and said to her, "I am going off to seek my fortune." "In that case," said her mother, "I will bake a bannock for you." When the bannock was baked, the mother asked. "Would you like the little bit and my blessing or the big bit and my curse?" "The big bit and your curse," answered the daughter. She took the way before her and when the night was falling she sat against a wall to eat her bannock. As she ate, there gathered around her the birdbeast and her twelve puppies, and the little birds of the air.

"Will you give us a bit of the bannock?" they asked.

"I will not give it, you ugly brutes. I haven't enough for myself."

"My curse on you and the curse of the twelve birds, and the mother's curse is the worst of all."

The eldest daughter got up and went on, not having had nearly enough with the bit of the bannock. A long way off, she saw a little house, and if it was a long way off she wasn't long getting there. She knocked.

"Who's there?"

"A good servant wanting a master."

"We want that."

So in she went. For wages she had a peck of gold and a peck of silver; and every night she had to be awake to watch a dead man, brother to the housewife and under spells. Besides that, she had the nuts she broke, the needles she lost, the thimbles she holed, the thread she used, the candles she burned, a bed of green silk above her, a bed of green silk under her, sleeping by day and watching by night. The first night she was watching she fell asleep. In came the mistress and struck her with the magic club. She fell down dead and the mistress threw her out behind the midden.

Up got the middle daughter and said to her mother, "I am going off to seek my fortune and follow my sister." Her mother baked the bannock, and the middle one chose the big bit and her mother's curse, and she set off, and everything that happened to her sister before her, happened to her.

Up got the youngest one and said to her mother, "I am going off to seek my fortune and follow my sisters." When the bannock was baked the mother asked, "Would you like the little bit and my blessing or the big bit and my curse?"

"The little bit and your blessing," answered the youngest daughter. She got that, and took the way before her, and when the night was falling she sat against a wall to eat her bannock. As she ate, there gathered around her the birdbeast and her twelve puppies and the little birds of the air.

"Will you give us a bit of the bannock?" they asked.

"I will that, you pretty creatures, if you keep me company."

She shared out the bannock, and they ate and they had plenty and she had enough. They clapped their wings about her till she was warm and comfortable.

The youngest daughter got up and went away. A long way off she saw a little house, and if it was a long way off she wasn't long getting there. She knocked.

"Who's there?"

"A good servant wanting a master."

"We want that."

So in she went. For wages she had a peck of gold and a

peck of silver, the nuts she broke, the needles she lost, the thimbles she holed, the thread she used, the candles she burned, a bed of green silk above her and a bed of green silk under her.

She sewed and sat watching the dead man. In the middle of the night he got up and screwed a grin. "If you don't lie down," she said, "I'll give you one wallop with a stick."

He lay down. After a while, he got on his elbow and screwed the grin. The third time he arose with the grin, she hit him one wallop. The stick stuck to the dead man, her hand stuck to the stick, and off they set. They went through a wood, and when it was high for him it was low for her, and when it was high for her it was low for him. The nuts were knocking their eyes out and the sloes hitting their ears off. When they got through the wood they went back to his house. There she received the peck of gold, the peck of silver, and a vessel of balsam. She rubbed the balsam on her two sisters and they came to life. They returned home, and (concluded Martha) they left me sitting here, and if they were well, it is well, and if they were not, let them be.

Martha lifted her arms a little, like two wings; her curved hands came down, cupping her knees; her head nodded up and down with monstrous rapidity.

The miller went towards her, complimenting her, and giving her at the same time a discreet look. From under her apron she withdrew a small bag and no word was said between them.

When the others were talking to Martha, the miller went away and filled the small bag with meal, and left it outside by the door. Then he came back where the merry words were flying.

At last Martha got up and said she would not be keeping them any longer from their work with her old foolish stories. "My blessings on you, and on this mill, and may its best doings be ever hid from the eyes of destruction." She went out and there was the little bag by the door. Putting it on her back, she set off for the small cabin where she lived alone.

Donul dug Art with his elbow. "Come on," he said softly, and put Art before him. Outside it was now nearly dark. "Give me your hand," said Donul.

Art gave him his hand and they walked along in silence. Presently Art asked: "Who is the birdbeast and the twelve puppies?"

"No-one knows," answered Donul.

"Are they all birds or are they all beasts?"

"No-one knows for certain. But that's the way they are in the story."

That made a difference. "I thought once or twice," said Art in a quiet voice, "that I just saw them."

"I have thought that myself sometimes," answered Donul. And then he asked: "What did you think they were like?"

Art gripped Donul's hand and in a low voice said: "I thought the birdbeast was like a great raven, and the puppies were like black puppies."

"I thought something like that myself," agreed Donul. "They are queer, anyway."

Thought of the queer engaged Art's attention for a little time. At last he said: "The machinery was quiet to-night."

"It was," nodded Donul.

"Was it doing nothing?"

"It was just lying in behind the walls."

"It would be dark where it was?"

"Dark as tar," said Donul.

"Does machinery sleep?" Art asked.

"No. It just waits."

"I know what it does," said Art. "It lies awake, waiting."

"Do you think so?"

"I do," said Art. "And then — and then — it springs with a roar and — and goes round and round."

"It goes," explained Donul, "when Kennie or someone puts the water on to the wheel. It waits for that."

"Does it?" said Art thoughtfully. And then he added: "And it always goes?"

"Always."

"And if you kept the water on the wheel, would it go for ever and ever?"

"For ever and ever," answered Donul.

"And all that time," said Art, gripping Donul's hand hard, "it's ready to drag you in?"

"It's the one thing it never forgets."

"Art!" called their mother's voice in the dark distance.

"That's Mother. Run! If they ask you, say I'll be home in a wee while."

"I'll say that," promised Art.

"You're not frightened of the dark for a little way?" asked Donul, his kind brother.

"I'm not frightened," declared Art. He started running as fast as his legs would carry him, shouting: "Mother, I'm here!"

George Mackay Brown was born in 1921 in Stromness, Orkney. He is a full-time writer. A born story-teller, he continues the rich tradition of which he is inheritor.

He attended Newbattle Abbey College when Edwin Muir was Warden; a most happy meeting, for that fine poet, a Shetlander, is of the same spiritual breed. Later he went to Edinburgh University.

In his introduction to the volume of stories, The Two Fiddlers, *from which this one is taken, George Mackay Brown writes: 'Orkney, Edwin Muir the poet said, is a land where the lives of living people turn into legend. . . . The islanders have always loved legends. In previous generations, on a winter night there was nothing else for them to do but tell stories and play their fiddles' (and both are very good occupations).*

These Orcadians and Shetlanders, although of different race and language from the Hebridean islanders whom Campbell knew, had their own, similar heritage which they treasured. They too knew sea-magic; and their special form of that was the seal legend. Seals, according to tradition, are of part-human ancestry, descending from a royal lineage.

THE SEAL KING

One day a rich merchant in Norway said to his only daughter, 'You have reached the age when you should be married.'

'O no, father,' said the girl. 'I don't want to be married. I don't want to leave home.

'And I am loth to lose you,' said her father. 'But the time comes to every girl. She must leave her father's door and go in at the door of her husband. Certain young men are coming to see me soon. No doubt one of them is fated to be your man.'

'I don't want a husband,' said the girl. 'I love to go with my hawk to the hill. I love to watch the wild swans on the lake. I love Thunder my horse. A husband would take me away from all that.'

The suitors came — handsome young men, wealthy young men, talented young men. They sat at the merchant's table and danced to the music of harps and pipes in the great hall.

The girl sat among them, silent. She danced with them but she kept her eyes on the floor. Her hands lay cold in their hot hands.

And when the love-sick young men looked again, she was gone.

She had taken her hawk to the hill. She was riding Thunder along the clattering mountain roads. The old peasants smiled at her as she went past, her bright hair streaming in the wind.

As for the suitors, they went home, disappointed, one after the other.

There was a young man in the north called Odivere. He was not so rich nor so talented nor so handsome as some of the other suitors, but he had what none of them had — a dark desperate courage.

He had heard about the rich girl and the suitors.

He determined that nobody but himself would put the golden ring on her finger.

How could it be done, seeing that he had none of the advantages of those others?

Odivere invoked the help of the kingdom of evil. He conferred with dark spirits. He struck a bargain with the magnates of hell. How it happened we shall never know now, but it is likely that Odivere went to a Black Mass, where black candles are burned and the crucifix is inverted and the Lord's Prayer is recited backwards. . . . When he came out from that terrible conclave, he had the assurance of his heart's desire.

In due course Odivere presented himself at the rich merchant's door. He was probably received coldly by the merchant. But when the girl, standing half-way down the stair, saw him, she put her hands to her rapturous mouth.

Odivere put on her a bold masterful look.

Later that day the merchant let it be known that he intended to give his daughter in marriage to Odivere, a rather poor knight from the north, that nobody had ever heard of.

After the wedding, Odivere took his bride to the gloomy hall where he lived. It was a lonely place, with no other great houses for miles around. The lady Odivere missed the busy commerce of the seaport, the chatter of the sailors, the subtle speculations of the merchants over this cargo and that.

But she resigned herself to her new life. It was not so much that she loved her husband as that she seemed bound to him by some powerful dark magnetism — she could not explain it.

She organized the work of the household as best she could. Once the pig was on the spit and the looms were humming and the washerwomen were busy at the pool, she was free to walk along the rocky coast where only sea-birds lived in the waves and crannies.

She loved especially to watch the coming and going of the seals. Often she whistled to them. Then they would pause from their fish-catching and turn their beautiful liquid large eyes on her. The seals love music.

These were the only animals she had now. If she thought of her hawk, and Thunder the horse, and the swans (white splashes on the dark tarn) pain touched her heart and drew tears down her face.

'If only,' she thought, 'I had a child — all this regret would be turned to happiness!'

But the years passed and she had no child.

As for Odivere, she feared him a little; and at the same time she felt herself owned and possessed utterly by him.

One morning Odivere announced to all his household

that he intended to go on a crusade. He had thought about it, he said, for a long time. There was little scope for his energies on his estate. In the east, there would be adventure under the bright sun. There was the certainty of loot and plunder. Besides, he said darkly, there, in the Holy Land, he might be able to atone for his sins, especially for one sin the memory of which haunted him night and day. Of course no-one dared to ask him what sin that was, so terrible that it seemed even Father Nord the household chaplain could not absolve him of it.

The lady Odivere begged him not to go. Her life, she assured him, would be utterly empty if he joined the crusade. Her spirit would wither in these gloomy walls. Her only consolation would be the skuas and the seals.

But Odivere had made up his mind. The day before he went he gave his wife a golden necklace as a perpetual love token, whatever should happen.

Then he rode south to join the ship of the crusaders.

She felt, for the first week or two, that all the meaning had gone out of her life. Then a stillness came on her spirit. And then, with spring — she could hardly believe it — a wild surge of joy the like of which she had never experienced since she left Thunder and the hawk and the wild swans. She was young again in the grey and blue and silver light of a northern spring.

She sang to the seals one morning. A bull seal turned his powerful head towards her. He surged towards her on a wave. She turned and ran, laughing, up the sand and the rocks to the herd-road above.

The slow hard cry of the seal followed her.

Halfway home, she looked down from the hillside to the shore. The seals were drifting still through the shallow waters. Where the great bull seal had blundered ashore a man was standing, his hand stretched up to her, in greeting and in supplication.

The years passed, and she could get no news of Odivere or of the crusade. One or two of the old serving-women in the hall shook their heads: they knew all about war and the things that happen in war: no doubt Odivere had been killed in some battle with the fierce Moslems.

A bull seal turned his powerful head towards her

And they shook their heads again — 'There's no son to inherit the estate.' . . . And they shook their heads yet again — 'And the widow, she's still young and sweet and beautiful. How sad it is!'

The absence of her lord had a strange effect on the lady of the hall. Sometimes her heart was wrung with a dark anguish for him. Sometimes the thought that he might never come home again made her sing and dance in the loneliness of her room. Either way, the violence of the emotion, when it came, frightened her.

She lived much of her life among the birds and seals.

Six years passed, and still Odivere had not returned.

There was a faint cry down at the shore one morning, 'A knight!' The lady heard it as she sat at her sewing. She got to her feet. The cry was repeated at the main gate, 'A knight!' She put down her needles and coloured wools and ran out into the courtyard. Her heart fluttered in her throat with joy and foreboding.

A knight stood at the main gate arguing with the porter. It was not Odivere.

'This man,' said the porter, 'says he has a message for you, my lady. He says he has news of Odivere. But every tramp and tinker that passes says he has news of Odivere. I'm tired of sending the liars away. I'm sorry your ladyship has been troubled again.'

The knight and the lady looked at each other.

'I have come from the walls of Jerusalem. I have a message to you from the lord Odivere.' His voice sounded like the muted thunder of a western sea, like cliff-cries and cave-echoes.

The lady Odivere invited the stranger with the sea-voice to enter her hall. She saw that there was a seal graven on his breastplate.

The laws of courtesy forbade the returned crusader to speak too frankly about Odivere and his doings in Palestine.

But it was a brutish picture that emerged from his careful words.

Odivere, it seemed, had done little or no fighting against the infidels. A brief first taste of war seemed to have sickened him. He and his men had soon gone north, to the splendid city of Byzantium. He had covered his going with some excuse, such as, that his services were urgently needed at military headquarters there.

But there were, in addition to headquarters, many less arduous places in the city — houses of pleasure, wine-shops, gardens with roses and stone cupids and nightingales. And it was in these places, in the company of the most scented and notorious ladies of Byzantium, that Odivere spent most of his days and nights. Over the years this cold northerner had gained a certain reputation as a gambler and a breaker of hearts (though the first flecks of grey were beginning to show in his beard). As for religion — and Byzantium had more splendid churches than any other city on earth — Odivere after a time did not so much as crook a knee or cross himself under any of those arches.

The day passed, while the knight told, as gently as he could, the lurid story of Odivere's crusade.

After sunset she went and lit a candle in the chapel, and came back again.

Still the sea-voice went on — Odivere at the gambling tables, the songs and the boastings of Odivere in the wineshops, Odivere among the little dark dimpling painted faces in the streets of pleasure. . . .

'I have heard enough,' she said. 'It seems that my husand is a famous man in the east. Do you think he will ever come home?'

'He will find it hard to tear himself away,' said the knight. 'But his money won't last forever. He is, in fact — I know it — deeply in debt to the money-lenders. Some dark night, when he can get no more out of them, he will slip away. He will whisper to some ship-master. Then the long journey home will begin.'

The lady Odivere lit a candle in her chamber; then another. It was growing dark quickly.

'I thank you for this news,' she said. 'It has hurt me, and yet it has given me a great happiness and freedom. You are most welcome.'

'Another winter, I think, and he will be home,' said the knight.

'As for you,' said the lady, 'it is too dark for you to ride home tonight, wherever your home may be. You will stay here in the hall till morning.'

The knight thanked her.

The lady Odivere blew out the cluster of candles on the table.

You have told me nothing about yourself,' she said — 'who you are or where you come from. But it seems to me that I have seen your face somewhere before.'

There was silence in the dark room. They heard only the thunder of the sea on the crags below, and, at midnight, the bad-tempered porter telling a stable-boy to slide the bar across the main gate. Nobody more would be entering or leaving.

The knight said that the lady and he had seen each other, many summers ago, down at the shore. The pain of her song had moved him. But he had not been able to bring her any comfort, for she had run away from the seal-dance. . . .

At first light the crusader left the hall and rode northwards.

Next winter a new baby, a boy, was born to a young fisherman and his wife who lived in a hut just outside the gate of the hall. This birth surprised all the folk of the village, because Norna had shown no signs of coming motherhood. Indeed, the day before the birth she had been stitching nets along with the other fish-women, as slim as a branch. The infant had suddenly appeared in a cradle, to the wonderment of everybody. The fisher folk know from bitter experience that the coming of children — though a blessed thing — makes the parents poorer and hungrier, for a time at least. This did not happen in the case of Thord the fisherman and Norna. On the contrary, little luxuries appeared in their hut; a woven coloured blanket, a looking-glass, a singing bird in a cage. . . . Thord was a rather lazy young man who more often than not stayed at home when the other fishermen were out saving their lobster creels from the storm. It made no difference — Thord and Norna and the infant ate whether Thord went out fishing or not. They seemed, in fact, to eat much better than the other fisher families. Neighbours observed — with jealousy or with curiosity or with smiles, depending on the nature of the observer — that often there were little honey-cakes on the table, and white bread, even an occasional flagon of wine. How could Thord and Norna ever afford such things? As for the boy, when he was old enough he ran about the doors like a little prince — all silks and silver buttons — not like a fisherman's child at all. Besides — even the jealous folk had to admit this — he was a marvellously beautiful child, with friendly winning biddable ways, so that even the bad-tempered porter bent down and stroked his bright curls whenever the boy reined his hobby-horse at the gate of the great hall. Thord and Norna were a coarse-looking pair — how on earth had they brought forth such an enchanting child? . . .

The lady Odivere was even more intrigued with the boy than the other folk of the estate — so much so that hardly a day passed that she did not visit the hut half-way down the cliff. And what was this? — the boy had full access to the hall as soon as he could walk — the porter had been given orders — whenever the boy knocked the bolt was slid and he passed through the courtyard and into the chamber where the women sat at the looms. The women too had been given orders. One of them would rise up at once and go to fetch the lady Odivere. Then — until her ladyship arrived, no long time — the weavers put kisses and gentle hands and kind wondering words on the young visitor.

Once, when he was six years old, the boy fell ill — some childish complaint that makes the patient thin and fretful and feverish but is soon over. The fisher folk think nothing of such things. Their bairns lie quiet in a corner for a day or two until presently they are mischievous and hungry again. But this boy of Thord and Norna's — he was positively cosseted back to health. It made the fisher folk laugh. It was not Thord and Norna that made fools of themselves in this way — it was none other than the great lady of the hall. As soon as news reached the hall that the boy was sick she hurried to the hut with a stricken face. There she stayed, day and night, for a week. She put slivers of ice between his lips in the early evening when the fever was at its height, she bathed his small white winsome body as least once a day. She worried about his lack of appetite — he was growing

137

thinner before her very eyes, she assured Thord and Norna
— she tempted him with little bits of pheasant from the hall
kitchen, and sips of French wine from the hall cellar. All to
no avail — the little patient turned his face to the wall — all
this fuss annoyed him — he wanted nothing but to be left
alone. The lady Odivere saw, for the first time, a frown of
annoyance on the child's face. It was as if he had put a
dagger in her. . . . In a few days, of course, the ruddy spots
left his body. He roused Thord and Norna one morning —
he said he was hungry — would they get him a bowl of
porridge, please? . . . That morning the lady Odivere was
beside herself with joy. The precious little creature was not
going to die after all. She lifted him up and covered him with
kisses. Thord and Norna turned away, embarrassed. (The
fisher folk love their children in a different way.) That night,
to celebrate his recovery, the lady Odivere brought a gift to
the boy: a golden chain. She put it round his neck. It
gleamed in the lamplight. The boy yawned — the gift did not
particularly interest him. But Thord and Norna clasped
their hands. That their humble home should ever contain
such a treasure!

To love a child is natural and good. The fisher folk show
their love in muted ways, not out of any emotional poverty,
but because they fear that any extravagant displays of
affection will rouse the envy and enmity of Fate.

The old women shook their heads. This would never do,
they muttered. That kind of love should never be lavished on
a child. There would come an end to it. This day or that,
Fate would present a reckoning.

It came as no surprise, therefore, to these old women
when the boy vanished suddenly one day. He was last seen
playing with stones and shells on the sea-verge. (The shore
had always been his favourite playground. He had learned
to swim when he was three years old. The sounds of the sea
were always in his mimicking mouth: the glut of ebb in a
cave, a blackback's shriek, shells' whisperings.) A
beachcomber was the last person to see the boy. He said that
there had been a herd of seals off-shore that morning, led by
a great grey bull. These seals had been there for a week and
more, he said, lingering and waiting and watching. When

the beachcomber had finally manoeuvred the heavy piece of driftwood ashore — the rib of a ship — he had turned for home. The boy, he said, was standing naked and waist-deep in the sea, looking outwards. There seemed to be no danger. When the beachcomber was half-way home he heard a great rejoicing shout. The sea rang and echoed from cliff to cliff. The herd of seals was making swiftly westward. The shore was empty. That did not worry the beachcomber either — the sea is full of noises — he simply thought that the boy, a sea-hunger on him, had gone home for his dinner.

But the boy did not come home for any meal that day, or the next day, or ever.

The searchers found a small linen shirt on the sand. They found breeches with a blue silk waist-band in the rock-pool. They found one sealskin shoe trundling back and fore in the breakers, as if it belonged half to the land and half to the sea.

The boy had been drowned. There was no other explanation.

The faces of Thord and Norna were muted with sorrow. For days they went about their tasks like people in a trance. Sorrowful faces came and stood in their doorway and uttered sorrowful words and went away. (Among the fisher folk it does not do to be too extravagant with sorrow either: lest a worse thing happen.)

But the lady up at the hall, who loved this lad so passionately and so foolishly (according to the standards of the common people) surely her heart must break, now that this stroke had fallen from the fist of Fate.

It did not happen that way.

When the news was whispered to her, fearfully, by Thord the fisherman, a look of wonderment came on her face, and she nodded. Then she asked humbly if Thord and Norna would let her have an article of his clothing — say, the little shirt. Then she said that she would like to speak to the beachcomber.

'It's shock,' thought the fisherman. 'She does not realize yet. Soon the truth will take her by the heart, and then the hall will be filled with a terrible outcry for days on end.'

But when Thord took his leave, having promised to let her have the shirt, and the breeches and the sealskin slipper too, she still had the tranquil look on her face.

She was smiling, the beachcomber said later down at the fishing boats, when he arrived. He was given ale and bread and cheese. He told, once again, the story of what he had seen. He had to tell it five times before she would let him go. It seemed she wanted specially to hear about the herd of seals. She was more interested in them brutes, and especially in the great bull seal, than she was in the boy, said the beachcomber.

At last, near nightfall, smiling, the lady sent the beachcomber away with a silver coin in his pocket.

Early one morning, a month after the sea-taking of the boy, there was a huge random clattering of hooves in the courtyard, and shouts, and cries.

The people in the hall ran to the doors, rubbing the sleep out of their eyes.

Horns were blown. A bell clanged.

Half a dozen men stood beside snorting pawing horses on the cobbles. They were dark with the sun; their teeth flashed in their faces. The porter was weeping with joy. It was Odivere. The lord Odivere had returned from his crusade.

Never had there been such excitement in that lonely northern hall. Servant girls ran to embrace the horsemen. Stable boys led the horses away. There were excited cries in the early morning, laughter, a few tears.

The fishermen were just about to launch their boats. They shouted a welcome from the shore.

Suddenly there was silence.

The lady Odivere had come to the door of the hall. Her husband looked at her eagerly. Servants and ostlers fell away. Odivere and his wife approached one another. They kissed in the courtyard. She stood on tiptoe and offered him her small cold mouth. So one offers courtesy to a stranger, between bits of more important business.

The first thing that Odivere did was to proclaim a holiday to celebrate their safe return from the east.

For three days nothing was done on that part of the coast. There was music and dancing in the courtyard. Fires were lit on the hill and on the shore. Ploughmen put away their shares and fishermen hauled their boats high up the noust.

The only busy place was the kitchen, where the cook and her helpers were kept at it roasting young pigs, and boiling fowls and fish, and baking and brewing.

Farmers and their wives and children came in from miles around to take part in the revels.

They hardly recognized their master. Odivere had been branded by the sun. His eyes and teeth flashed in his face whenever he was moved to mirth or rage; which seemed to be more often than in the old days. The young children who had only heard his name up to now ran frightened into their mothers' skirts whenever that vivid face looked at them.

Father Nord said a Mass for the safe return of the crusaders from the Holy Land. The whole community crowded into the chapel, but it was noted that Odivere was not present.

Feasts and holy days star the rustic calendar. These celebrations in a poor countryside are welcome and necessary. But once the feasting is over there are bare cupboards to be stocked again, by hard toil from dawn to dark.

After three days of festival the boats were launched and the yoke was put on the oxen. Then the dogs had their feast of bones.

For Odivere and his men it was difficult to return to the old routine. They had been away for twelve years, spending their strength on exotic business. It would take some time for these adventurers to bend their minds and bodies to the old yoke.

One thing was certain, however — they could not lounge about in the courtyard for ever, drinking idle ale. It was a rather poor estate — everybody from the highest to the lowest must work, or starve.

'Well, lads,' said Odivere to the gypsy faces who had gone crusading with him, 'the great adventure is over. Now it's back with us to the old monotonies of sea and land.'

The sun-dark faces nodded glumly all around him.

'We're going to have one last fling, all the same,' said Odivere. 'That three-day feast — look how fat we are after it. It will never do. Today we're going otter hunting along the coast. That will get us back into condition.'

141

The Jerusalem-farers all stood up and cheered. Then they went into the great hall to fetch their weapons.

The otter-hunt was not a great success. The hunters were — as Odivere had said — fat and out of condition. The otters flowed away from the flung spears. The hunters grunted and panted after elusive animal dances. At the end of an hour they all sat down on the rocks, wiping their brows.

In the old days, before the Holy Land, they had been able to match their cunning against the cunning of otters, and win as often as not. In twelve years they had forgotten many skills.

It was a disconsolate company that sat among the rocks that morning.

A sleek head broke the sea surface twenty yards off-shore — a young seal. The hunters eyed it dully. Apart from the fact that they could not hit it, it was — they knew — bad luck to kill a selkie.

Odivere stood up. He drew back his arm. His hunting spear flashed in an arc from shore to sea. There was a commotion in the water — a scream — a writhing — a red froth. The seal, transfixed, was thrown ashore on the next wave.

The hunters cheered in a half-hearted way. They looked at each other uneasily.

Two of them went down to the verge to retrieve their master's hunting spear.

One of them cried out in amazement.

He took from the neck of the young seal a gold chain. He held it up. It glittered in the sun.

The lady Odivere was sitting with her women at the tapestry frame. They heard a disturbance at the door. Odivere strode in. The women, all except their mistress, cried out — they had never seen so terrible and stricken a face. Odivere flung what seemed like a sodden sack on the clean pine floor. But when they looked again it was a young seal with rags of blood about its shoulders — a red tattered cape.

'Tell me, woman,' said Odivere, 'what is that?'

'A dead seal,' said his wife. 'I thought you were after

otters."

'And what is this?' said Odivere, and held out the gold chain.

'It is a gold chain,' said the lady. Her face was as white and stricken as Odivere's now, but her voice was like his too, quiet.

'It is not just any gold chain,' said Odivere. 'It is the gold chain I gave you before I left on the crusade. It was to be a token of undying love between us.'

One by one the women left their threads and needles and crept away into the kitchen. But they kept their ears to the curtain.

'Your love did not last long once you left home,' said the lady Odivere. 'How many painted women did you give gold to in Byzantium?'

'I loved you, woman,' said Odivere. 'I loved you more than any of them. And what I did in the east — all these small flirtations — that was natural, what a lonely man is entitled to. But what were you up to when I was away? And what is this?'

And he kicked the dead seal towards his wife.

The lady Odivere bent down and embraced the sea-creature. She kissed the snout and the glazing eyes and the torn throat. When she looked up again her grey dress was all red and clotted.

'It is a seal. It is a young dead seal. But it was not always a selkie. Once it was a beautiful boy that used to play in this very chamber. Never has the coast seen such delight and such winsomeness. I think even you, you evil man, would have smiled to see him at his stories and rhymes and games. But now he is dead.'

The rage had died in Odivere. He stood there, in the hall of the women, overcome by a lassitude that no amount of rest would cure — a life-weariness. Nothing would ever matter to him any more.

'You have killed my son,' said the lady Odivere to the broken man.

A few days later the lady Odivere was tried in a hastily-convened district court. She refused to say whether she was guilty or not guilty of the fearful crimes she was charged

143

with. She never uttered one word from the beginning of the trial to the end.

But there was evidence enough against her. Thord the fisherman and his wife Norna admitted that they had been well paid to foster a new-born child that one of the women had carried down one midnight from the great hall. The porter described the overnight stay of a knight who claimed to have a message from Odivere to his lady: this knight had had a seal graven on shield and breastplate. The little silk jackets and the slippers of Spanish leather were held up for all the court to see.

The lady Odivere listened and looked with a cold face.

Before nightfall the district court had found her guilty. She was condemned to be burned to death in the courtyard next day at noon.

The body of the seal had lain meantime in a corner of the courtyard, overlooked in the fear and excitement and consternation that fell in waves upon the estate during those terrible few days.

But on the day of the trial Odivere ordered one of the ostlers to bury it at the shore.

When the ostler bent to pick up the selkie the pelt came away in his hands. He found himself looking at the cold white body of a boy. He looked closer; it was Thord and Norna's son, the lad who for a year or two had put a kind of happy innocent enchantment on the coast.

What should he do? Should he tell Odivere, or the priest?

Odivere was in no state to be told anything. Since the otter-hunt he had gone around like a man half-crazed. The smallest thing — like a jug of milk accidentally spilled — roused him to violent rages. Two days previously he had gone into the smithy where some of the farm labourers were eating their midday bread and cheese, and had launched into a lurid story of one of his exploits in Palestine: how he had challenged an Arab to a duel, on account of some fine desert girl that they both fancied, and how after a desperate fight he had pulled the Arab from his horse, and taken out his knife. . . . There, at the climax of the boast, he had broken off, and looked blankly from one rustic face to the other, and then left as suddenly as he had come in. Only yesterday the ostler-gravedigger had come on him in the stable — he was sitting in the straw, laughing to himself, and sniggering, as if life and time were a great joke. And he had not been aware of the stable-man's presence either. . . .

So the man went to Father Nord's door, and whispered to him, and pointed. Father Nord crossed himself, and muttered some Latin. Later that evening the seal-child got a lonely burial beside the church.

Now it was the morning of the execution.

The roads to Odivere's hall should have been crowded with folk, all trooping in to see the burning; for Odivere had proclaimed another holiday, another feast.

But the roads were empty.

And the fisher folk stayed at home right enough, but they shuttered their doors and remained inside.

In spite of the terrible things that had been said about her at the trial, the whole countryside had come over the years to love the lady Odivere.

There was likely to be only a straggle of louts and sadists round the stake at noon.

But at first light an unexpected excitement broke. The look-out on the cliff reported that there was a school of whales off-shore, spouting and wallowing and shouldering the sea apart.

'Whales! Whales!' This was the most exciting cry that could be heard on any northern coast. The whole community — women as well as men — gathers on the shore. Every available boat is launched. Every available weapon, even ploughs and scythes, is carried. The boats make a great wide circle round the whales. The women scream and bang saucepans and tongs. Girt with such terrible din, the whales turn in the direction of silence, which is the shore. One by one the terrified creatures hurl themselves on the rocks and sand. There they are cut to pieces with the knives of the hunters. Stone jars are filled to brimming with oil. Let the corn die, that coast will not starve next winter. A hundred huge red whale-steaks are carried to this cottage and that, to be smoked and salted; but most of the meat will of course find its way to the kitchen of the hall.

This was the usual pattern of a whale-hunt. But this

particular school of whales seemed endowed with special cunning. Odivere and his people tried time and again to outflank and encircle them; and time and again, at the last minute, the whales blundered into the west. The whale-hunters were drawn further and further out to sea. And again, Odivere ordered an outflanking of the school; but · soom foolish woman clashed her pans too soon, and then the half-encircled whales made new sea-quakes westward.

'We will try once more,' said Odivere. 'It will soon be time for the burning.'

Fifty oars flashed in the sun.

We earth-dwellers will never know the huge sympathy that binds together the creatures of the sea: so that when a terrible wrong has been committed, a single pulse of pity beats through the cold world-girdling element, and seal, pearl, whale, and sea-blossom devise with their God-given instincts that which will restore beauty and wholeness to the breached web.

While man and whales pitted their cunning against one another, far out, near the horizon, one by one, subtly and silently, the seals foregathered and came ashore; and suffered the earth-change; and stood as tall handsome men among the rocks.

They drifted into the empty hall where the lady Odivere lay in a black cell, with chains at wrist and ankle, waiting for the fire at noon. The seal-men unravelled the chains — they fell clanking to the floor. The seal-men carried the woman down to the beach. The host entered the water. They led the lady Odivere to the kingdom of Imravoe, the seal king who had waited so long for her.

Very far west that kingdom lies, beyond the Orkneys, half-way to Atlantis.

As they swam into the deeper sea, their voices rose and fell among the spindrift and the hovering skuas:

'I am a man upon the land,
I am a selchie in the sea,
And when I'm far from any strand
My home it is in Sule Skerry.'

Bibliography

Buchan, John, *Witch Wood,* Hodder & Stoughton
(London, 1927)
Campbell, Lord Archibald (ed.), *Waifs and Strays of Celtic
Tradition,* 5 vols., David Nutt (London, 1889-92)
Campbell, J.F., *Popular Tales of the West Highlands,* 4
vols, Alexander Gardner (Paisley and London, 1890-3)
Campbell, John Gregorson, *Witchcraft and Second Sight in
the Scottish Highlands,* James MacLehose & Sons
(Glasgow, 1902)
Gunn, Neil M., *Young Art and Old Hector,* Souvenir Press
(London, 1976)
Hogg, James, *The Tales of James Hogg, The Ettrick
Shepherd,* 2 vols, Adams & Co. (London and Hamilton,
1884)
Kirk, Robert, *The Secret Commonwealth of Elves, Fauns
and Fairies,* The Observer Press (Stirling, 1933)
McKay, John G., *More West Highland Tales,* 2 vols, ed.
W.J. Watson and others, Oliver & Boyd for the Scottish
Anthropological and Folklore Society (Edinburgh, 1940
and 1960)
Mackay Brown, George, *The Two Fiddlers: Tales From
Orkney,* Chatto & Windus (London, 1974)
Oliphant, Mrs Margaret, 'The Secret Chamber',
Blackwood's Magazine, December 1886
Scott, Sir Walter, *Letters on Demonology and Witchcraft,*
George Routledge & Sons (London, 1884)
Stevenson, Robert Louis, *The Merry Men,* Chatto &
Windus (London, 1916)
Wodrow, Robert, *The Analecta, or Materials for a History
of Remarkable Providences, mostly relating to Scotch
Ministers and Christians,* Matthew Leishman for the
Maitland Club (Edinburgh, 1842/3)